The Gambia and Its People:
Ethnic Identities and Cultural Integration in Africa

Godfrey Mwakikagile

Copyright © 2010 Godfrey Mwakikagile
All rights reserved.

The Gambia and Its People: Ethnic Identities and Cultural Integration in Africa
Godfrey Mwakikagile

First Edition

ISBN-13: 978-9987-16-023-5

New Africa Press
Dar es Salaam, Tanzania

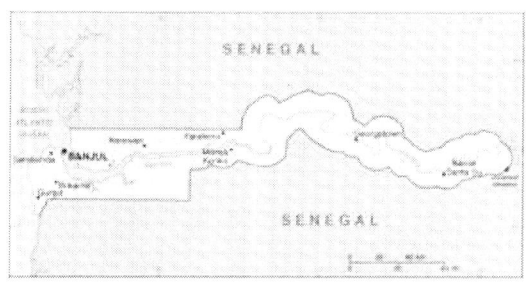

Introduction

THIS work focuses on one aspect of The Gambia: the people and their ethnic identities and cultures.

It also provides a comprehensive picture of the country's nation identity which is a fusion of the multiple identities of the various ethno-cultural groups which collectively constitute the Gambian nation.

In spite of its ethnic and cultural diversity, The Gambia is one of the most united countries in Africa. It's also one of the most peaceful, enjoying harmonious relations among its various ethnic groups unlike many African countries where instability and civil strife caused by ethnic rivalries – fuelled by unscrupulous politicians – is the defining feature of national life.

The ability of the various ethnic groups in The Gambia to interact harmoniously has also led to cultural integration on a scale unheard of in most African countries. While it's true that different tribal cultures do exist in The Gambia, it's equally true that there also exists a national culture which unites the country's various ethnic groups into a cohesive whole transcending ethno-regional loyalties.

As an ethnically diverse nation, The Gambia is a microcosm of Africa: a continent whose countries are characterised by ethnic and cultural diversity where rivalries along tribal and regional lines are the norm rather than the exception. But The Gambia also is a good example of what many African countries have yet to be: united, with a solid national identity that has not been fractured or fragmented by ethnic conflicts.

Cultural integration on a national scale has remained an elusive goal in most African countries since independence. But if there are a few countries on the continent which have achieved cultural integration, The Gambia is one them. It has, in fact, even achieved cultural fusion in some respects as we learn from this work which focuses on Africa's smallest country and its people.

The work is intended to be a general introduction and may help members of the general public learn some important things about The Gambia which, because of its strategic location and other attributes, has earned distinction as a gateway to West Africa.

The People and The Culture of The Gambia

THE GAMBIA has a number of ethnic groups or tribes which collectively constitute the Gambian nation.

The country has eight major ethnic groups. And there are smaller groups which are equally important as an integral part of the nation.

Smaller indigenous groups include the Badibunka, the Balanta, the Bambara, the Bayot, the Hausa, the Mandjak, the Mankanya, and the Mansoanka.

We are going to take a look at them in general and focus on those which are broadly representative of the country as a whole in terms of culture and demographic composition.

The Mandinka, Malinke or Mandingo, are the largest. They constitute almost half of the entire population. And they are broadly representative of The Gambia in many fundamental respects, a status attributable to their numerical preponderance and the role they have played in the establishment and evolution of The Gambia as a nation.

Their language is the most widely spoken indigenous language in The Gambia.

The Wolof are another major group. Although they're the third-largest after the Mandinka and the Fula, they are highly influential in many areas of national life. They're also the dominant group in the Banjul urban area.

Some observers believe that Wolof will one day become the lingua franca of The Gambia, replacing Mandinka.

In addition to being the main local language across the country, Mandinka is also dominant in the rural areas, and Wolof in the urban areas.

Many Gambians, especially in the urban areas, also mix English with local languages, a phenomenon that has led to the creolisation of the English language especially among the Aku, an ethnic group composed of descendants of freed slaves.

Many Akus are also descended from interracial relationships between Europeans and black African women during the slave trade and through the years thereafter including the colonial period.

The mixture of English with local languages is also common in other parts of Africa. For example, in Tanzania where Swahili is the dominant language, many people, especially the educated, like to use English words and phrases when they speak Swahili, a practice that has led to the development of what is now known as Kiswanglish, although it has not acquired the status of a separate or distinct language the way pidgin English or Creole has in many parts of West Africa.

But before we look at each of the Gambian ethnic groups in some detail, we're going to take a look at The Gambia as a nation from a cultural perspective and try to see how the people across the country live in general, especially in their traditional societies.

Cultural Landscape: An Overview

It's probably not an overstatement to say that some cultural fusion has taken place in The Gambia through the centuries even before the country was created by the British. That is because of the close cooperation and interaction including intermarriages among the different ethnic groups inhabiting the area that came to be the country of Gambia as we know it today.

Another strong binding force is Islam. The people of Gambia are also united by Islam not only as a religion but as a way of life. Islam is a religion. But it's also a way of life which has helped the people of Gambia to forge a common identity and a united nation.

It's also equally true that each ethnic groups has its own customs and traditions and other practices in spite of this cultural integration. Yet there are cultural elements probably among all the ethnic groups which are a product of cultural fusion that has taken place through the centuries among the different tribes in the area of Gambia and probably in the larger region of Senegambia as a whole.

In some cases, cultural affinity has historical roots. For example, the Wolof and the Serer share a common ancestry, as do other groups, even if they took different paths afterwards. Besides the language, Serer customs are also similar to Wolof customs, an affinity that has helped to foster, maintain, preserve and promote harmonious relations between the two groups.

Harmonious relations are sometimes a product of interdependence. Different groups of people are not self-reliant all them time. They need each other. This leads to a close relationship attributed to survival, but also quite often simply to love and respect for each other.

The close cooperation among the different ethnic groups in The Gambia, and the oneness of Gambians, is also demonstrated by the fact that many Gambians feel closer to fellow Gambians from different ethnic groups than they do to their fellow tribesmen in neighbouring Senegal and other countries in the region.

For example, the Wolof constitute the largest ethnic group in Senegal and the third-largest in Gambia. They straddle the Gambian-Senegalese border. Yet not all members of the Wolof ethnic group in Gambia feel closer to their kinsmen in Senegal than they do to fellow Gambians of other tribes.

They feel closer to fellow Gambians regardless of the tribes they belong to. The same applies to other Gambians whose ethnic groups straddle the Gambian-Senegalese border and whose members also live in other countries such as Guinea and Mali.

It's an attribute many Gambians share and one of the most important attributes of their national character and identity. It also shows how Gambians live as individuals and as a nation. It also reinforces their cultural identity as one people which transcends ethnic loyalties.

But even this cultural identification of Gambia as a single socio-political unit has not eliminated ethnic distinctions in terms of identity and was never intended to. The existence of tribes or different ethnic groups is an integral part of African identity in any African country especially south of the Sahara. Therefore elimination of tribal or ethnic distinctions through a deliberate policy of social engineering would be a disaster and a negation of African identity.

These distinctions extend to other spheres and areas of life including the way people earn a living. For example, in The Gambia, the Seharuli are heavily involved in local trade. In fact their name, "Serahuli," is virtually synonymous with "traders."

They're also farmers and live mainly in the Basse

region in the eastern part of Gambia. They're also the newest ethnic group in the country. They fled from religious wars in Senegal and settled in Gambia in the 1800s. Their dialects include Azer and Kinbakka. They're also known as Serahule.

The Jola are known for the cultivation of rice and live mostly in Fula District in the Western Division. Living in virtual isolation in deep forests and swampy areas, they were among the last people in The Gambia to embrace Islam.

The Fula are known for cattle ownership although there also large numbers of sedentary Fulas, making both pastoral and sedentary living an integral part of the Fula culture and way of life. They have strong cultural and historical ties with the Tukulor. The Tukulor are mostly farmers and livestock owners.

The Serer – sometimes known as Serere – have a reputation as fishermen and as boat builders. They're prominent in coastal areas. And together with the Jola, they are believed to be the oldest inhabitants of the area that came to be known as the country of Gambia.

The Mandinka, mostly engaged in farming, are among the most well-known people in West Africa who excel as griots. They're also known for their music which has ancient roots. And the *kora*, one of the musical instruments they use, is considered to be a symbol of Gambia's national culture and identity.

The Wolof who live on the north bank of the Gambia River are mainly farmers. And those in the Banjul area are prominent in business and in the civil service. The Wolof are also renowned for their griot tradition common among many ethnic groups in different parts of West Africa.

Other groups are known for different activities. But one of the most important aspects of Gambian national life is that all these activities – interests, roles and specialties – transcend ethnic boundaries even if some groups are identified with specific social and economic functions more than they are with others. A lot of this has to do with the close cooperation the people of different ethnic groups have enjoyed for centuries, in spite of the conflicts they have had in their long history in the past.

Centuries of intermingling including intermarriage has also led to a situation where different ethnic cultures and "the national culture" overlap, with many aspects of tribal cultures assuming a national character. It's a phenomenon that can be described as the universalisation of tribal cultures in Gambia's cosmopolitan context, while at the same time creating a truly national culture with distinct characteristics.

Some of the main aspects of Gambia's national culture have been identified and described by Ebrima Colley, a Gambian, in "Gambian Culture Notes":

"Many ethnic groups... in The Gambia...share enough cultural patterns that...appl(y) to the majority of the country's people....

Greetings are a most essential aspect of Gambian culture. Many foreigners who have lived in a village can attest to the amount of time spent going through the greetings when one Gambian meets another during the day....

People are taken aback if you do not greet first before beginning a conversation even if you just want to ask a question....

Greeting in a local language is recommended – *salaam alekum* – but an English 'Hello' will do. For foreigners, these greetings may seem a meaningless waste of time because they are always the same and quite lengthy.

You may also be baffled to see a Gambian doing something you consider 'really important' stop everything to spend ten minutes greeting a friend he has seen just hours ago. But once again it is because greeting acknowledges the existence of another human being and taking the time to relate to him or her in a personal way is a priority in Gambian society which helps achieve the goal of harmony and peace in the community.

Every member of the community is expected to greet every other member of the community regardless of status or wealth. Indeed, the greetings are a way for the Gambian to show respect for every member of the community whether they are rich or poor, noble or of slave origin, because every member has an important role to fulfill.

Shaking hands is also a part of the greeting process. People shake hands as often as they see each other during different times of the day. Women, especially in villages, are not normally expected to shake hands when greeting.

When greeting a group of people or someone from a distance, raising clasped hands will take the place of a handshake.

When one is working or eating, the arm may be offered instead.

Gambians follow a certain protocol for greeting elders: a younger person greets an elder first and avoids direct eye contact.

Also, physical affection for a loved one or emotion in general is not openly shown in public. Note that in shaking hands the right hand is used. The left hand denotes something else...." – (Ebrima Colley, "Gambian Culture Notes," St. Mary's College of Maryland, St. Mary's City, Maryland, USA, 2002, pp. 1).

The Muslim greeting – *salaam alekum* – is universally accepted as a local greeting because Gambia is a predominantly Muslim country.

The greeting is in the Arabic language which is the language all Muslims use worldwide as the language of the *Qur'an*, the holy book for Muslims.

But there are equivalents of the greeting in the indigenous languages which you can use if you know them.

Here are a few examples:

Hello – *Kairabe* in Mandinka; *Nakam* in Wolof.

How are you? – *Ibe Nyaadi?* in Mandinka; *Jamun Gam?* in Wolof.

I am fine – *Mbe Kairato* in Mandika; *Jama Rek* in Wolof.

Good morning – *Isama* in Mandinka; *Naka Subaci* in Wolof.

Good afternoon – *Itinyau* in Mandinka; *Naka Beket Bi* in Wolof.

Good evening – *Iwurara* in Mandinka; *Naka Ngonci* in Wolof.

What is your name? – *Itoudi/Itodun?* in Mandinka; *Nakaga Tuda?* in Wolof.

My name is Momodou – *Ntomu Momodou Leti* in Mandinka; *Sama Tur Momodou La* in Wolof.

Good night – *Suto Yediya* in Mandinka; *Fanan Jama* in Wolof.

Good-bye – *Fowati Koten* in Mandinka; *Ci Jama* in Wolof.

Farewell – *Foo Watido* in Mandinka; *Be Bennan Yon* in Wolof.

The examples given above come from the two main local languages spoken in The Gambia. And they should be enough to exchange greetings with most of the indigenous people in the country.

Most Gambians speak Mandinka or Wolof or both languages in addition to their tribal languages, for example Jola or Serahuli or any of other languages if they're not members of the Mandinka or Wolof ethnic groups.

Greeting someone is extremely important in Gambia and in other African cultures. It's considered rude, very rude, not to greet someone. It's also taken as an insult when you just start talking without first greeting the person you want to talk to.

It's as a bad as refusing to accept food when you are invited to eat with members of a household. Many people also feel that you think you're better than they are if you refuse to eat with them.

They also feel that you think their food is dirty and they themselves are dirty. Unfortunately, there is some truth to that in many households all over the world including the most developed parts such as Europe and North America.

So, you have to be very careful. It's a minefield. How you handle it, depends on what kind of society you are in and what kind of people you're dealing with. In some cases, it can be very dangerous.

People take insults very seriously. Fortunately, if you are in a country like Gambia which is known for its peace and harmony, you don't have to worry about being attacked simply because you refuse to eat the food you have been offered by the indigenous people. As Ebrima Colley goes on to explain how Gambians handle delicate situations, for example, when they are offended by some one:

"It is also interesting to note that Gambians often express anger, not by hostile words or threats, but by refusing to greet the person. This is considered a great insult denoting a lack of respect or outright contempt for the individual. This is important to remember since in other societies a 'hello' and a wave of the hand are enough to show the pleasure you get from seeing someone.

If a Gambian villager is asked why he spent so much time greeting, repeating the family name over and over, he would reply that he is not only saying the name of the individual with whom he is speaking, but that he is also acknowledging that person's entire family, and the history of the family, the ancestors as well as the living.

Foreigners living in The Gambia (especially in a traditional village) must realize then that they may hurt people's feelings by not greeting every individual with whom they come into contact even if the other is in the middle of a business transaction, a discussion with someone else, reading, etc.

This can be exasperating if the foreigners don't understand the capital significance the greeting ritual has in Gambian society for showing concern for the well being of the individual and his family circle.

The foreigner may think nothing of walking into an office and saying point blank 'I need this or that,' because in his society he is trying not to waste the other person's time and to get straight to the point.

This foreigner may wonder why Gambians are so slow to help him out – or even seem a bit hostile – even though it may be their job. However, the Gambian feels he has not been acknowledged before getting down to what he considers secondary matters." – (Ibid., p. 2).

These are matters of cultural sensitivity. If you don't take the time to learn basic customs and practices in the country, the indigenous people will conclude that you have no respect for them and for their society and way of life. You can't get things done.

You may not even be able to get any help, because of that, if you need some help. The people may simply ignore you.

The generosity of Gambians is demonstrated in many ways even if they don't have enough to eat. They share with others including foreigners whatever they have, however little.

When you go to a house and you see that the people are already eating or they're getting ready to eat, you're automatically considered a diner. They're going to share the food with you. They don't ask you whether or not you want to eat something the way, for example, Americans ask. They just invite you to join them to eat.

This is common not only in The Gambia but in other African countries as well. I know this because I am an African myself, born and brought up in Africa.

But there are also rituals to be observed and followed even when you're simply getting ready to eat. They differ from society to society. In The Gambia, as Ebrima Colley explains:

"The most common way of eating in The Gambia is from a communal bowl. A mat – or mats – is spread and the bowl is centrally placed on the mat. Before you sit on the mat it is polite to take off your shoes – as you always do before stepping on a mat.

Look to see how the men and women sit and do likewise. In an average compound, especially in rural areas, men eat from one bowl and women from another.

Children are divided between bowls according to sex; at times boys eat with the men.

If you arrive when people are eating you are immediately invited to join them. It is considered polite to wash your hands and 'taste' the food even when you don't feel like eating.

If you do not want to continue eating you should leave the eating area and wait until they are through as it is considered impolite to watch people eating.

If you are visiting a village or compound for the first time, you may be served in a separate hut all by yourself, as a compliment to show the importance they give to you!

The meal is usually brought out in a large bowl and if there is sauce, it is poured out from a second bowl by the female head of the house.

Hands are washed before and after a meal from a communal basin.

Even if one is left-handed, the right hand is used for eating.

Usually you will be offered a spoon, which you should not hesitate to use although joining the group in eating with one's hand is a welcome gesture.

It is best to wait for the host to begin the meal by saying '*Bisimillah*.' This is the equivalent of saying 'Grace before the meal' and means 'in the name of God' in Arabic, the official language of the Moslem religion.

Hosts are expected to distribute the pieces of meat, fish, or vegetables to the rest of the group. The bowl is invisibly divided into sectors with each person eating from the portion directly in front of him/her. You can also reach out for the meat, fish, or vegetables that are usually in the center of the bowl." – (Ibid.).

Some people may find this to be distasteful. But that's how things are done. And that's how the food is eaten, of course, in The Gambia.

There are other rules to be observed and followed. For example, you're not supposed to talk when you're eating. This rule is even more strict for children. Talking while eating is considered to be bad manners. Also, there are superstitions which are invoked to discourage people from talking when they're eating.

Sometimes, adults may say a few words, for example describing the food as being hot. But when they say "the food is hot," they don't mean it's hot because of hot pepper; using hot pepper is an integral part of food preparation in The Gambia and in many African countries. They say the food is hot when it's really hot in terms of heat, not taste from hot pepper.

There are also other cultural differences, for example, between The Gambia and the United States, concerning table manners.

One has to do with belching which many Americans and Europeans may consider to be distasteful or bad manners. As Ebrima Colley who emphatically states from experience as a Gambia explains:

"It is not considered rude to belch; on the contrary it is an indication that you have eaten well and your host will be pleased." – (Ebrima Colley, "Gambian Culture Notes," ibid., p. 3).

It's exactly the opposite in the United States and probably in many – or perhaps in most – European cultures. Many people in those parts of the world consider that to be rude; not so in The Gambia and in many other African countries. It's just part of the process when you're eating.

Also, traditionally, Gambians don't like being watched by someone they don't know when they're eating. They fear the "evil eye."

To avoid that, they invite everyone to eat, although the main reason why food is offered to everybody is hospitality, one of the most important attributes of the Gambian way of life. But you don't have to accept the invitation if you real mean well, and you are not doing so out of contempt, when you refuse to eat:

"If one does not want to eat one should say 'thank you' and avoid watching those eating.

Occasionally your host will insist that you eat despite your repeated declining of the invitations. He is just being polite and will leave you alone if you are adamant, but remember to either leave the area or occupy yourself with something else, e.g., reading a book. Depending on the familiarity with your host and the practicality of the situation you may not actually leave the eating area." – (Ibid.).

One of the major differences between Gambians and Westerners is that women in The Gambia don't eat together with men. They eat separately. And that's common in many African cultures including mine, Nyakyusa, except among those who have been exposed to Western culture through modernisation including education.

But even among westernised Africans, a very large number of them stick to tradition not only in The Gambia but in other African countries as well. They believe in gender separation, which some people, especially Westerners, may say it's a euphemism for male chauvinism.

As in other African countries, wives in Gambia even have separate houses, especially in the rural areas, and don't live in the same house with their husband. But this practice is not strictly enforced in urban areas because of modernisation and even for practical reasons: lack of ample space to have separate houses, and financial constraints, among other things.

With gender separation and gender roles is the dress code. But the dress code does not apply just to women; it also applies to men.

Africans in general are known to be very conservative in attire, especially in traditional settings, and frown upon those who want to show parts of the body which are supposed to be covered. For example, I remember in the 1970s when some countries literally "declared war" on people wearing mini-skirts and those who bleached their skin. They included Tanzania, Malawi, Zambia, and Guinea.

It's a stereotype and an insult when non-Africans say Africans don't like to wear clothes or that they like running around naked. In most cases, you are not going to see that in African countries including Gambia where traditional attire is highly cherished:

"In traditional Gambian society, a garment should cover most parts of the body. The garment should fit loosely so that the shape of the body is not revealed. Men wear 'haftaans and warambas,' which are long gowns with elongated armholes worn over baggy trousers.

Women also wear haftaans as well as warambas worn with a wrapped skirt or blouse underneath. Younger women can be seen wearing a distinctive close fitting tunic with a plunging neckline and matching wrapped skirt made from cotton prints.

In the urban areas, European style clothing is commonly worn. Although certain dress styles may be unique to one ethnic group, these clothing styles are worn interchangeably by everyone....

Warambas and haftaans are often made from tie-dye or batik damask and are embroidered in elaborate designs.

Sarongs as well as shorter warambas are also made from the locally woven strip cloth that comes in multi-colored strips between four and eight inches wide.

The white strip cloth woven up country is made with local cotton or imported thread.

While women usually wear head ties that match their dresses, men often wear wool hats, skullcaps or a fez, especially on religious occasions." – (Ibid.)

Besides traditional attire, another very important thing which distinguished Gambians and other Africans from other people is hair style.

Hair style, especially for women, is very important in African traditional societies and even among urban dwellers. For example, you are not going to find a single African country south of the Sahara where people, mostly women, don't braid hair. Look at The Gambia:

"Hairstyles are a work of art in The Gambia. Women braid and plait their hair, often using fiber extensions in intricate and ornate designs....

Gambian women wear earrings, necklaces and pearls. Gold and silver ornaments are also popular.

Gambian women are as modest as they are elegant. Modesty in dress is very much an influence of Islam.

The thighs of a woman are to a Gambian man what the breast is to a foreigner (*tubab*), and thus not exposed.

Wearing pants, even long ones, is considered inappropriate by tradition.

Although bare breasts are not considered immoral or provocative among Gambians, women do not normally walk with bare breasts outside their compounds unless they are working or breastfeeding." – (Ibid).

Compounds are the basic social units of the Gambian traditional society. And they have survived modernisation. No amount of foreign influence has been able to weaken let alone destroy this social structure.

It's strongest in the rural areas where the vast majority of Gambians live and where traditional institutions are very strong. There is social cohesion in the urban areas as well. But it's in the villages in different parts of the country where you are able to see the real Africa – hence the real Gambia – in its "pristine" state and beauty.

Social stratification is patrilineal in the Gambian context. Men, heads of households which are called compounds in The Gambia, wield enormous influence over those under their jurisdiction: family members, usually their wives and children and, quite often, relatives who live there.

This social pattern is also common in most parts of Africa where most families are patrilineal. And The Gambia is a typical example of that:

"Despite the gradual erosion of traditional culture through urbanization, The Gambia's social organization still retains much of its traditional character, especially at the village level....

The basic social unit in the village is the family that lives together in an area called a compound, hence, compound family. It consists of a compound head, his wives, children and other younger males with their wives and children.

The head of the compound is the eldest male and is legally responsible for everyone in the compound. He is also the chief mediator of all disputes and the first to be consulted on any major event or responsibility involving the family.

Every compound family belongs in a clan or ward in the village of related compounds built near one another, forming a small neighborhood. The head of the clan is also the eldest living male of the related families.

The eldest male of the founding family of the village becomes the chief or *Alikaaloo*. The leaders of the clans who are responsible to the Alikaaloo form the council of elders, which serves as the village's governing body together with the *Alikaaloo*." – (Ibid., p. 5).

Gambia also has some elements from the past when the structure of the society was hierarchal, composed of those who were free, those who were artisans, and those who were domestic slaves.

This structure defined one's social status and determined one's roles and rights in society. The stratified nature of the society also made it almost impossible for members of different social classes to marry. A slave couldn't marry a free man, although it happened sometimes. Still, it was not encouraged, and such taboos were more often than not strictly enforced.

But a lot of that has changed, although the past is still present because of the conservative nature of the various tribal or ethnic communities in the country.

Many people in The Gambia are aware of their social origins and prefer to marry people of similar background, an attitude reinforced by the conservative nature of tribal communities, especially in the rural areas.

Yet they're receptive to foreigners and even to some changes which don't undermine their traditional way of life. This way of life is maintained and reinforced in many ways, one of which is the use of traditional items to strengthen social ties.

One of the most important items used that way in traditional societies in West Africa is kola nuts. Kola nuts are offered as a symbol of hospitality. They're also offered as a gesture of friendship and to show respect. They also symbolise peace.

It all depends on the purpose. But they're highly significant in West African traditional societies from Nigeria to Gambia, Ghana to Mali. The list goes on and on.

They have been so important in those traditional societies that they also symbolise wealth. There was a time when they were even used as a form of currency. Even today, they can be easily exchanged for other items on traditional markets in West Africa.

Kola nuts are also used in arranging marriages. In The Gambia and other West African countries, the family of the bridegroom send kola nuts to the family of the bride. If the bride's family accepts the kola nuts, it means they expect things to go well.

In The Gambia, the people including elders or community leaders appreciate kola nuts just as much:

"The *Alikaaloo* also gives shelter and hospitality to strangers who know no one in the village....The offering of kola nuts to the Alikaaloo and hosts is the traditional way of introducing oneself and is a gesture of respect." – (Ibid., p. 6).

Another very important figure in the Gambian society is the *Imam*. It's an Arabic word. *Imam* is a religious title in the Islamic faith.

The *Imam* conducts prayers in the mosque. He also serves on the council of elders in the village.

This dual role enhances his status, especially in a society which is predominantly Muslim.

The respect accorded an *Imam* is equivalent to the respect a priest or a minister gets from Christians.

The importance of the *Imam* in a community in The Gambia also reflects the conservative nature of the society. Islamic societies are known to be very conservative, and traditional communities in The Gambia are no exception.

The conservative nature of the traditional society, where little has changed in terms of customs and traditions including marriage customs, is clearly demonstrated by the prevalence of arranged marriages in the country.

Although many people in urban areas don't adhere to these customs and practices, and some of them even frown on arranged marriages, the practice is widespread in traditional societies where it's also highly cherished as a basis for social order, as a bond of kinship, and as respect for the traditional way of life which has been practised and upheld for centuries going all the way back to the days of "our ancestors."

Even child-naming ceremonies are important. They're traditional. And they're common in The Gambia. Usually, it's family members on the father's side who name the child.

Another very important practice is circumcision. It's an integral part of the initiation ceremony and it's common in many parts of West Africa, not just in The Gambia. As Ebrima Colley explains:

"Circumcision in many West African societies is a rite of passage that is part of the life cycle that mark the beginning of adulthood.

Boys and girls are circumcised separately in groups between the ages of 8 - 12, although some participate in the practice at even an earlier age.

Circumcision of girls is still practiced among the Mandinkas, Fulas and Jolas, but not among some Wolofs.

Children would traditionally spend several months in the bush with a special guardian for general training after the operation.

During their healing period in the bush, they are taught about their adult social responsibilities and rules of behavior.

While boys wear distinctive white robes with a triangular hood, girls wear a special dress adorned with strings of beads.

Great preparation is made in the village for the returning children. Parents make beautiful clothes and decorations for the new initiates to wear for several days after their return.

The ceremonies associated with initiation are marked by much feasting, socializing, and special dancing with masquerades, e.g., 'kankurangs' - this is a masked figure that appears during important ceremonies.

Today most people in the urban areas take their children to the hospital or clinic for the actual operation and the bush school lasts for a shorter period." – (Ebrima Colley, ibid., p. 7).

Even with the intervention of modernisation, for example the use of hospitals to blunt the effects of circumcision, the practice still persists; so do bush schools where those who have been circumcised in hospitals still go even when it's for shorter periods.

Modernisation has not been able to stamp out the practice, an enduring testimony to the resilience of the African spirit when it adheres to customs and traditions. As the saying goes, habits die hard. In this case, it's even harder, much harder, for customs and traditions to die after they have survived for centuries.

The way the people mourn the dead is another traditional practice that has endured. And it's not different from the way other Africans mourn. For example, members of my tribe, the Nyakyusa, wail loudly just like the people in The Gambia, thousands of miles away, do. They also alert other people if someone has died just like Gambians do, showing that Africans from different parts of the continent have a lot in common in the way they live traditionally:

"Loud wailing and sobbing – mostly by women, is a common way to express sympathy to a mourning family in

The Gambia.

When a person discovers a death in the village, he or she will alert the rest of the community with a loud death wail.

Elders will make burial arrangements and send messages to inform kin folk and friends. The body is washed and clothed in a white shroud and is rolled in a mat or placed in a coffin.

The body will either be brought to the mosque for prayers or will remain in the compound before the burial, which usually takes place after the prayers. The men take the corpse for burial.

After that, charity is also customarily given to the mourning family in the form of money or food.

Another charity by the family of the deceased takes place on the third, seventh and fortieth days after the burial.

The mourning period for a widow in traditional Muslim practice is four months and ten days. During this time, the widow is supposed to remain inside the compound and not dress fashionably. This practice is to ensure that if the widow is pregnant, the husband's family will know that the child belongs to their lineage. A widower, however, does not follow a mourning practice." – (Ibid.).

Another thing – among many others – Gambians have in common with other Africans is wife inheritance. When a man dies, his brother can inherit his wife or wives. People of my tribe, the Nyakyusa, do that but the practice is now rare. I heard about it when I was growing up but not much. The point is that it was for a long time an integral part of Nyakyusa culture as much as it is of Gambian society today.

The brother of the deceased also assumes the role of father to the children left behind by his brother. It's all a part of the extended family way of life but with an added component of inheriting wives. The extended family is one of the solid foundations of traditional societies across Africa.

Africans are also known for their hospitality. Gambians are no exception. They give gifts during various ceremonies, not just weddings. Even when they travel, they take gifts to the people they're going to visit; a practice also common among my fellow Nyakyusa tribesmen, especially women.

Nyakyusa women almost invariably take some food with them, usually a large bunch of green bananas or a basket of maize balanced on their heads, when they go to visit someone, near or far, or when someone has given birth to a child.

Gambians give all kinds of gifts including kola nuts, the traditional item for hospitality. They also support each other in times of disaster, for example, a flood or a fire.

But don't give gifts, or take or accept anything with your left hand. Don't greet people with your left hand. And don't eat with your left hand.

It's taboo, not only in The Gambia but also in many other parts of Africa. People of my tribe, the Nyakyusa, have the same rule against using the left hand. It's reserved for cleaning yourself up after you attend the call of nature. I remember that very well when I was growing up. I was born left-handed but my father forced to learn how to use my right hand.

But there are somethings you also don't do with your right hand. Don't point your finger at people in The Gambia and in most parts of Africa, including mine. It's highly offensive to many people in most traditional societies in Africa. I remember many young people who were chastised for pointing their fingers at people when I was growing up.

The different aspects of life shown here clearly demonstrate that there are many things Gambians of all ethnic groups share in terms of culture. And they collectively constitute what may be called Gambian national culture.

It's essentially a multicultural society. It's also multilingual. Most Gambians speak at least two indigenous languages, one being their own. And it's not uncommon to find those who speak more than two tribal languages.

But although the country has one "national culture" which is a product of cultural fusion through the years and even centuries in some cases, the cultures of the different ethnic groups are equally important. In fact, it's from these diverse cultural groups that Gambia as a nation derives her richness in cultural diversity while at the same time integrating the various cultural elements, from different ethno-cultural groups, to create a synthesis of Gambian national culture whose essential features – at least some of them – we have just seen here.

As I mentioned earlier, there are eight main tribes or ethnic groups in The Gambia. And they all live together in peace and harmony while respecting the distinctive characteristics and unique identity of each group.

Even the cultural fusion that has taken place through the centuries has not been able to erase or eliminate the distinctions between and among these groups. Each has its own customs and traditions, language and music and other distinctive attributes which give each group its own identity and that's unique in several respects to make it different from the rest.

Yet there's no question that the colonial experience – hence colonial culture – which lasted for more than 200 years has had a profound impact on Gambia's national life. And since culture is a way of life, the colonial experience has therefore become an integral part of national culture but also in a way many people don't even realise because they simply take it for granted as their way of life.

This can be easily seen in the Anglo-Saxon traditions which permeate different areas of national life, including individual lives, in Gambia which are in sharp contrast with what goes on in Senegal where French culture has played an equally decisive role, if not more so, in shaping the national culture and the lives of the Senegalese, especially the elite, even turning some of them into black Frenchmen.

Still, the mere existence of the different ethnic groups and their ways of life even in the face of this onslaught by the imperial powers who propagated their cultures in their colonies at the expense of the indigenous people is strong testament to the resilience of the African spirit, values, customs and traditions, and ways of life through centuries of domination by Europeans who did a very good job teaching Africans that they had nothing to offer to the rest of mankind in terms of civilisation.

Besides the main ethnic groups – Mandinka, Fula, Wolof, Jola, Serer, Serahuli, Manjago, and Aku – there are other groups. But they are smaller and not officially acknowledged probably because they settled in The Gambia only recently, compared with the other groups which have lived in the country at least for more than 100 years.

The smaller indigenous groups are Balanta, Papel, Susu, Jalunke, Mankaan, and Mansuwarka.

There is another group, or it can be said there used to be another group, called Bayinunka. It was one of the oldest tribes in the region of Senegambia. But it's almost extinct. There are no people who speak the Bayinunka language anymore. Those who still exist and who can identify themselves as Bayinunka have already been assimilated into larger groups and no longer claim their distinctive identity. They also speak other languages as their primary languages, mainly Mandinka and Jola.

But their brethren still exist in the Casamance Province in southern Senegal and in the former Portuguese colony of Guinea-Bissau which borders Casamance. And they still speak the Bayinunka language.

The ethnic groups which exist in Gambia today are inextricably linked with other groups in neighbouring countries. They share historical and cultural ties with the people of Senegal, Mali, Guinea, Guinea-Bissau, and Sierra Leone. In fact, most of them migrated to what is now Gambia from other parts of West Africa.

That's why they share ethnic ties and many cultural values, customs and traditions with the people in those neighbouring countries. They're basically the same people separated only by national boundaries drawn by the colonial rulers who partitioned Africa.

The migratory pattern clearly shows this common identity and where the people who now live in The Gambia originated.

The Mandinka, of the old Mali empire, once dominated the whole area from the north bank of the Gambia River to the Fouta Djallon, or Futa Jallon, a mountainous region in west-central in Guinea. They're also one of the major ethnic groups in Guinea and are found in many other parts of West Africa.

In Guinea, the Mandinka are called Malinke. In Liberia, they're known as Mandingo which is also probably their most well-known name especially to the outside world; it's also one of the most well-known names for tribes or ethnic groups in Africa like the Zulu, the Masai (really Maasai), the Ashanti, the Kikuyu, the Hausa, the Igbo and the Yoruba, among others.

In Mali, the Mandinka are called Bambara. And in the Ivory Coast and Burkina Faso, they're known as Jula.

It's only in The Gambia where they're officially known as Mandinka.

The second-largest ethnic group in Gambia, the Fula – also known as Fulani, Fulfulbe, Pulaar, or Pul – may have ancestral ties to the Berbers in the northern part of Africa. Like the Berbers, the Fula have a light complexion and somewhat straight hair. Many have just straight hair. Even some with dark skin have straight hair. Others have wavy hair. But their origin is still in dispute.

They look like Ethiopians. And some claim they

originated in the Arabian peninsula. But there is no proof of that. The origin of the Ethiopians – at least some of them such as the Amhara and others – is also believed to be the Arabian peninsula.

Ethiopians such as the Amhara, the Tigre, the Tigrinya and others in Ethiopia, have Semitic roots. They also speak Semitic languages which are related to Hebrew and other Semitic languages including Arabic. Ethiopians are also sometimes called "Black Jews," for example, in Libya and in Egypt.

But the Fula or Fulani language is not Semitic, although there are claims the original language may have Semitic roots or is related to Semitic languages.

In fact, some Fulas or Fulanis who have visited Ethiopia or who have met or have seen Ethiopians anywhere in the world say they look so much like the Ethiopians and believe they came from Ethiopia.

One possible explanation of their origin is East-North-West migration. It's possible they migrated from Ethiopia in East Africa to North Africa where they mingled with the Berbers before finally settling in West Africa.

The fact that they speak a language related to some West African languages does not preclude this possibility. And it does not necessarily mean that their origin is somewhere in West Africa.

After living in West Africa for centuries, they may have lost their original language and incorporated into it words, phrases and other linguistic elements from the languages of their neighbours in the western part of Africa, and even of the Berbers.

This may be only a theory but it's worth exploring because it has been validated in some cases.

One of the best examples is the migration of the Tutsi probably from Ethiopia to what is now Rwanda and Burundi in the Great Lakes region of East Africa more than 400 years ago. When they settled among the Hutu in those two countries, they gradually lost their original language. Now, all the people in both countries speak basically the same language: Kinyarwanda in Rwanda, and Kirundi in Burundi, both of which are closely related.

Many Tutsis have also retained some of their physical features – long faces, pointed noses, a light complexion, and a thin frame – which remind one of the Ethiopians and even the Somalis, in spite of the intermarriage that has taken place between the Hutu and the Tutsi for centuries, blurring ethnic distinctions.

In fact, in many cases, it's impossible to distinguish them based solely on the way they look; although it's also easy in many cases to tell – "That's a Tutsi" just from the way a person looks.

Therefore the fact that the Fulani look like the Ethiopians should not be entirely discounted or ruled out as proof of their Ethiopian origin. Further investigations – including DNA tests – should be conducted to establish whether or not the Fulani are related to the Ethiopians and if they really came from Ethiopia as many of them believe they did.

Belief by itself is not enough when dealing with scientific evidence. In this case, to be credible, it must be supported by science if there is scientific evidence to back it up.

Some Fulanis may believe they originated in Ethiopia. But if there is no scientific evidence or any other proof to support their claim, their belief will be just that, a belief, without any proof that's where they came from.

What's known, at least in the West African context, is that the Fula or Fulani have lived in the region of northeastern Senegal for a long time at least since 400 A.D. And they are believed to have originated there. Their language is also closely related to Wolof and Serer.

In The Gambia, they live mainly in the central, eastern, and northern parts of the country. Although they're known for their livestock, especially cattle, and many of them are farmers, they're also involved in other economic activities including commercial enterprises. Many of them own small shops.

There is also a lot of archaeological, historical and linguistic evidence which shows that the other groups in The Gambia also have a West African origin, although in the beginning they all came from East Africa. But after that, they consolidated themselves in West Africa where they have lived for many centuries.

One of the major groups in The Gambia, the Wolof, are believed to have migrated from southern Mauritania. The biggest wave of migration took place during the religious conflicts in the 1800s when the Wolof settled in the area that later became the country of Gambia. Their biggest stronghold was the area that's now Banjul and the north bank of the Gambia River. They earned a reputation as traders and as boat builders. The Wolof are also known as the Fanafa on the northern bank of the river.

The Jola entered Gambia from the wetlands of the Niger River and introduced rice, cotton and palm seeds into the country. Although they're one of the main ethnic groups in Gambia, especially in the coastal region, they're also a major tribe in Casamance Province in Senegal and in Guinea-Bissau. They're also known to be the most traditional people in Gambia in terms of religious practices, sticking to their tribal beliefs, in spite of the fact that most of them are Muslim. Some are Christians.

The Serahuli entered Gambia only recently in the 1800s as shown earlier. But they have a noble history. They were once the rulers and merchants of the old Ghana empire. Apart from being farmers and traders selling a variety of items including gold and diamonds, they're also known as excellent weavers of strip cloth, and as pottery makers which they highly decorate.

The Serer, one of the oldest groups in The Gambia together with the Jola, migrated from an area north of the Senegal River and settled in the northwestern part of the country. Although they're now dominant along the mouth of the River Gambia where they're engaged mostly in fishing, they also move from place to place following the fish wherever and whenever they migrate to other parts of the river.

The Serer also have ancestral ties to the Jola. And besides linguistic similarities, the Serer also share cultural ties with the Fula.

The Manjagos migrated to Gambia from the coastal region of Guinea-Bissau. They were migrants workers, working as seasonal workers in Senegal and Gambia. And some of them settled in the coastal regions of Gambia and Casamance Province. They're farmers but are also known for producing palm oil, making palm wine by tapping oil palms, and for rearing pigs.

All these groups have West African origin, coming mostly from the countries close to Gambia.

The only group of Africans in Gambia which has other origins as well is the Aku. They're Creole and first settled in Freetown, Sierra Leone, in 1787 before some of them migrated to Gambia in the 1800s.

As descendants of African slaves, there's no question probably the majority have a West African origin since most of the slaves who ended up in America and in Europe, especially in Britain, came from West Africa. But because they're also descendants of slaves, some of them have ancestral roots in other parts of Africa.

Not all slaves were taken from West Africa. Others came from Congo, Angola, and other parts of the continent including East Africa, especially Tanzania and Mozambique. Only a few were taken from East Africa but the exact number is not known and it's impossible to make a good estimate.

What's is known is that after the anti-slavery patrols intensified on the West African coast following the abolition of the slave trade in Britain and in the United States, slave traders turned their attention to East Africa, mainly what is now Tanzania and Mozambique. And

American ships, as well as others, were seen in Zanzibar during that period waiting for their cargo of slaves to take to the Americas.

Historical records in the United States also show members of some tribes in Tanzania and Mozambique who were taken as slaves to the United States. Some records on slave auctions in Louisiana were cited by *The New York Times* in the late 1990s and mentioned members of the Makua tribe – found in southern Tanzania and northern Mozambique – who were sold as slaves in the state of Louisiana in the southern part of the United States.

Therefore, the Aku in The Gambia, just like other descendants of African slaves elsewhere, can not pinpoint exactly where their African ancestors who were taken as slaves came from; although there's a highly probability that they came from West Africa since that was the main source of slaves during the slave trade. But other parts of Africa – including East and Central Africa – can't be ruled out as the origin of some of their ancestors.

Many Akus who are racially mixed are also a product of unions between African women and Europeans, including traders, who settled in Africa or who simply went there, and stayed for some time, for commercial purposes.

And although most Akus are Christian and have European names because of the strong European influence in their lives including the Western values freed slaves who settled in The Gambia and in Sierra Leone brought back Africa, some of them are also Muslims.

They also live mostly in the Banjul area, the most urbanised part of the country which is virtually an outpost of Western civilisation in the country.

And because of the dual identity of some of the Akus, as a product of Western civilisation and predominantly Islamic Gambia, some of those who are Muslim have first Muslim – Arabic – names but European surnames.

In Sierra Leone, the people who are called Aku in The

Gambia are known as Krio or Creole. And a very large number of Akus in Gambia are descendants of Creole immigrants from Sierra Leone.

It should also be remembered that the people in West Africa migrated from East Africa – including the Great Lakes region and other parts in the eastern part of the continent – thousands of years ago, probably about 5,000 years ago. And the people in East Africa today migrated from West Africa, especially from what's now eastern and north-central Nigeria – the Benue Plateau – and Cameroon about 2,000 years ago. Some also came from other parts of West Africa. So, basically, all these people have the same origin.

In the case of Gambia, the different ethnic groups have now formed a homogeneous whole in terms of national identity. But they have not fused to create an organic whole. Each group has retained its identity without compromising its place in the country as an integral part of the nation.

Ethnic Groups and Their Cultures

The existence of different ethnic groups or tribes is one of the most distinguishing features of African countries. Even in a country such as The Gambia where the people have achieved cultural fusion in some areas, major differences still exist among the different groups in terms of culture. For example, not all of them have the same beliefs in the traditional context dealing with religion, marriage rituals and other matters.

Indigenous religious systems differ in fundamental ways, although Islam has virtually supplanted them. But they still exist. And they differ from tribe to tribe.

The Jola are probably the most well-known group who adhere to their traditional religious beliefs with tenacity, although the vast majority of them are Muslim. There are also Christians among them even though they constitute only a small minority as much as they do in other indigenous groups.

Therefore, The Gambia is a heterogeneous society in spite of the fact that it has achieved a degree of national cohesion unparalleled in most African countries with the exception of a few such as Tanzania, Botswana, Swaziland, Lesotho and others although it should also be remembered that the vast majority of the people in the last three countries belong to one tribe – the Tswana in Botswana, the Swazi in Swaziland, and the Basotho or Basuto in Lesotho – with Tanzania being the exception where there are about 130 different ethnic groups, none of which enjoys numerical preponderance over the others.

Tribal or ethnic identity is also expressed in other ways, mostly cultural, including traditional authority. Traditional institutions of authority differ from tribe to tribe.

The existence of different traditional institutions among the various ethnic groups in The Gambia is also demonstrated by the fact that some of them still have caste systems, although the stratified nature of these traditional societies is not as rigid as it was in the past. But castes do exist. And many people respect these differences, with a significant number of them preferring to marry within their own caste, and so on.

This is especially true in traditional societies which are more likely to observe these differences because of the conservative nature of these societies.

Younger people, especially in the urban areas, don't pay much attention to these distinctions. But even they are aware of the differences which exist among the different tribes in The Gambia.

Each tribes has its own language, its own music and traditions and customs, identifying features which give legitimacy to group identity although not necessarily to the exclusion of – or at the expense of – other groups.

But even though these groups have their own identities, it's equally important to realise that they're mostly social categories and not biological entities. The tribes are not strictly biological units because of the intermingling which has taken place through the years, probably inter-tribal marriage being the paramount factor.

The people have intermarried through the centuries, cutting across tribal lines, resulting in the creation of societies which can not claim to be pure in terms of tribal identity.

Also, a lot of migrations have taken place through the centuries. Many people from different tribes in other parts of the region of Senegambia and beyond have been absorbed by the tribal communities in The Gambia, becoming an integral part of those societies.

One of the main factors which inspired and facilitated such migrations was trade, besides wars and natural calamities including drought and problems like land shortage and overpopulation which forced the people to move elsewhere. As Professor Boubacar Barry of the History Department at the University of Cheikh Anta Diop, Dakar, Senegal, states in his book *Senegambia and The Atlantic Slave Trade*:

"Senegambian societies, made up of domestic communities ranging from villages to states, were by no means autarchic, even if the subsistence economy played a very important role.

As a whole, Senegambia was integrated into a regional and long-distance inter-regional trading system. To start with, there was the exchange of agricultural products for dairy products, fish and handicraft products. The complimentary interactions of these economic sectors was a permanent reality that determined the operations of local or inter-regional trading circuits.

Cereal trading between the sedentary populations of the Senegal River valley and the Berbers of present-day

Mauritania was particularly important.

At the same time, there was a lively trade in fish, mainly from the mouth of the Senegal River to the upper Valley, where it was traded for millet.

A second circuit led to the rice-producing Southern Rivers. There was also the inter-regional trade in cola, cloth, indigo dye, and iron bars, transported through the Southern Rivers toward the savanna and the Sahel.

As a rule, trade in agricultural and handicraft products, as well as in produce gathered wild, went on between zones producing and zones needing them. The result was a complementary economy involving the varied exchange of produce from the savanna, the Sahel, the mangrove swamps, and the forest.

This inter-regional trading system linked Senegambia with three major trading zones: to the north with the trans-Saharan trade; to the east with the Sudanese trade along the Niger Bend; and finally to the south, with the forest trading circuits of Sierra Leone." – (Boubacar Barry, *Senegambia and The Atlantic Slave Trade*, Cambridge University Press, 1997, p. 32.)

This pattern of trade also led to inter-cultural relationships and exchanges and eventual assimilation of members of some groups by some of the people they interacted with. And as Boubacar Barry goes on to state:

"Senegambia is a transitional zone between the Sahara, the Sudan, and the forest belt. The region exhibits a measure of economic, political and social unity symbolized by the millet and milk diet of the north, the related rice and palm oil culture of the Southern Rivers, and the fonio and milk diet of the Futa Jallon plateau.

This peasant culture runs parallel to the cultural influence of the *khalam*, the *kora*, and the *jun-jun*, musical instruments imparting a characteristic beat to the daily lives of these societies situated at the junction of so many diverse influences from the Sahara, the Sudan, and the forest.

Though economically rather independent of each other, each with its subsistence economy, these societies were by no means isolated from each other. Individuals and groups did a great deal of traveling in all directions. When they reached a different community, they intermingled according to the rules of their host communities, in a region where there was still plenty of space for incoming migrants.

In the process, people switched ethnic groups and languages. There were Toures, originally Manding, who became Tukulor or Wolof; Jallos, originally Peul, became Khaasonke; Moors turned into Naari Kajor; Mane and Sane, originally Joola surnames, were taken by the Manding royalty of Kaabu.

There was, in short, a constant mixture of peoples in Senegambia, destined for centuries to share a common space. Senegambia, in some respects, functioned like a vast reserve into which populations in the Sudan and the Sahel habitually poured surplus members.

In their new home the immigrants created a civilization of constant influx, in which ethnic identities were primarily a result of the mutual isolation of domestic communities caused by the subsistence economy.

Nowhere in this Senegembia, where population settlement patterns assumed stable outlines as early as the end of the fifteenth century, did any Wolof, Manding, Peul, Tukulor, Sereer, Joola, or other ethnic group feel they were strangers – (ibid., pp. 34 – 35).

However, that was not going to last forever. The rise of European imperialism was to have a profound impact on these traditional societies and in a way that would change the destiny of the entire continent:

"From the late fifteenth century, this common destiny,

related to Senegambia's role as a transition zone, or even as an outlet for the Sahel and the Sudan, changed profoundly. Up until then, Senegambia's Atlantic coast was of little significance.

Then contact with the European maritime powers gave it unprecedented importance. That contact brought about deep economic, political, and social transformations. From now on the pre-capitalist societies of Senegambia came under pressure from a Europe in the full force of its capitalist expansion.

From that point on, it becomes impossible to understand the development of Senegambia without factoring in the impact of the European trading system, an external factor which monopolized exchanges between Africa, America and Asia by conquering the international market." – (Ibid., p. 35).

While European conquerors deliberately encouraged and fostered divisions among different African tribes to facilitate imperial rule and consolidate their power, their divide-and-rule tactics did not always succeed. They did succeed in solidifying ethnic identities to some degree. But Africans continued to interact even if not as extensively as they did before because of the constraints and restrictions imposed on them by colonial rulers.

And what had already taken place through the centuries could not be undone.

Therefore, because of all the interactions which had taken place through the centuries, the indigenous people had achieved a degree of integration – through commercial intercourse, migration, as well as intermarriage between members of different tribes – which could not only be undone or neutralised by the Europeans; it formed the basis on which Africans built nationalist movements in their quest for independence from colonial rule.

So, there are no pure tribes or ethnic groups, not only in The Gambia but in other parts of Africa as well.

But there are distinct tribal or ethnic groups, with their own identities, even if they're not pure. And most of them want to preserve those identities.

People from other tribes who have been assimilated become members of the tribes which have absorbed them and identify themselves as such.

If they are Mende from Guinea and become a part of the Mandinka traditional society, they become Mandinka in terms of ethnic identity. They adopt Mandinka values; they speak the Mandinka language, observe Mandinka rituals, and uphold Mandinka customs and traditions.

And in our survey of Gambia's cultural landscape from tribe to tribe, we are going to start with the Mandinka who are not only the largest ethnic group in The Gambia but one of the largest in West Africa and on the entire continent.

Mandinka

The Mandinka or Malinke are also known as Mandingo or Manding or Maninka.

Probably their most well-known name outside Africa is Mandingo.

They speak the Malinke language of the Mande branch of the Niger-Congo family.

Besides The Gambia, they also live in large numbers in Guinea, Mali, Ivory Coast, and Senegal.

Others in substantial numbers are found in Burkina Faso, Sierra Leone, Guinea-Bissau, Liberia, Ghana, and Chad, in that descending order.

About 99 per cent of them are Muslim. Although they're mostly farmers, they're also known to be very good fishermen.

Historically, they had a caste system. Vestiges of the system continue to be some of the identifying features or characteristics of the Mandinka society even today in sharp contrast with some of the other traditional societies in The Gambia.

The Mandinka are also have a long history in the area that's now Gambia. And their caste system not only shaped their society in a profound way; it also had a major impact on its destiny and that of the entire region dominated by the Mandinka; a point underscored in a book co-authored by Professor Arnold Hughes, director of the Centre of West African Studies at the University of Birmingham, and Professor David Perfect, in the United Kingdom, *Historical Dictionary of The Gambia*:

"The Mandinka have long been resident in The Gambia, probably moving into the area in the late 13th or early 14th centuries. They were certainly fully established on both banks of the the Gambia River by the 15th century.

Mandinka society was divided into three endogamous castes – the freeborn (*foro*), slaves (*jongo*), and artisans and praise singers (*nyamolo*).

Age groups (*kaafoolu*) were important in Mandinka society, in contrast to the sociopolitical organizations of neighborring Wolof people.

The basis of life for the Mandinka was, and is, agriculture, although they were also the dominant traders on the Gambia River.

In the second half of the 19th century, cultivation of groundnuts became the major activity for most Mandinka male farmers (women have tended to cultivate rice).

By 1800, the Mandinka provided the ruling class – and most of the inhabitants – of all bar one of the 15 kingdoms below the Barrakunda Falls.

Rule in each of these states was based upon kinship, and each king (*mansa*) surrounded himself with a complex of bureaucracy.

The kingdoms were subdivided into the territorial units of the village, ward, and family compound.

Village administration was carried out by the *satee-tiyo* (*alkaaloo*) in council. Each village was further divided into *kabilos* (wards), which were administered by a *kabilo-tiyo*, chosen on the basis of his lineage as well as his abilities.

The kings each maintained an armed force to defend the state and impose their will on their subjects. Because they were not themselves permitted to lead troops, the rulers chose a general (*jawara*) for this function.

The Mandinka systems of rule were challenged in the later 19th century by proselytizing teachers who wished to convert the Mandinka to Islam.

The ensuing conflicts led to the Soninke-Marabout Wars, which resulted in the breakdown of traditional Mandinka authority structures in the Gambia and the conversion of most Mandinka to Islam. With rare exceptions, most notably D.K. Jawara, few Mandinka converted to Christianity." – (Arnold Hughes and David Perfect, *Historical Dictionary of The Gambia*, The Scarecrow Press, Inc.; Fourth Edition, 2008, p. 141).

President D.K. Jawara himself returned to Islam and changed his first name from David to Dawda.

Even in this era of globalisation which has witnessed the spread of Western values and civilisation even further than before, most Mandinkas are still Muslim. Christianity has done little to penetrate the Mandinka traditional society.

And while Islam is sometimes considered to be "native" to Gambia and many parts of Africa because it has existed there for so long, its counterpart, Christianity, is not.

Christianity is also equated with Western civilisation and even with colonialism or imperialism since it helped pave the way for the colonisation of Africa. As Jomo Kenyatta once said: "The white man came and told us, 'shut your eyes, let us pray.' When we opened our eyes, it was too late. Our land was gone."

Therefore on the Mandinka cultural landscape,

Christianity is an anomaly, sharply contrasted with Islam which is an integral part of Mandinka culture.

The Mandinka traditional society has also been known for its ability through the centuries to accommodate and elevate some slaves in a way they never would have been had its caste system been rigidly enforced.

Slaves constituted the lowest social class. Yet many domestic slaves became an integral part of the families for whom they were worked and were even treated as true family members.

Even today, the people who are descended from these castes are aware of their historical position under the caste system which determined their social status, conferred rights and privileges, and determined their fate.

They lived within prescribed limits, including restrictions and prohibition against intermarriage between members of different castes; a phenomenon that still exists today in some cases. According to a work by some Gambians and others, *Sunjata: Gambian Versions of the Mande Epic*:

"The 'jali' as a social institution dates back at least to the time of Sunjata (also known as Sundiata), and has been, and remains, a cornerstone of Mande culture.

Mande society consists of three broad social categories: the *horon* (Mandinka: *foro*), who are the 'freeborn' – roughly equivalent to nobility – descended from rulers, and not attached to any particular occupation; the *nyamakala* (Mandinka: *nyamolo*), those who are born into certain professions or trades, for example music and other specialized verbal and performance arts (the jali); and the *jon* (Mandinka: *jong*), descendants of slaves and captives.

There is, still today, little intermarriage between these groups, which represent a form of social hierarchy, with the *nyamakala* in the middle." – (Bamba Suso, Banna Kanute, et al., *Sunjata: Gambian Versions of the Mande Epic*, Penguin Classics, 2000, p. xvi).

Several other tribes in The Gambia had the same system. And they all have remnants from the old social order.

Also, as in almost all traditional societies across the continent, men are the decision makers in Gambia. The social structure starts with the family.

The husband, father or eldest male member of the family is the head of the household. And his decisions are final within the family unit, an arrangement some African women, especially educated ones, equate with male chauvinism.

But the majority of them accept this arrangement because it fosters family stability. And it's in keeping with African culture, reinforcing African identity.

After the head of the household is the head of the village. And above him is the chief. The chief is assisted by a group of elders or an elders' council.

Arranged marriages are also common in the Mandinka traditional society.

Polygamy is an old institution in traditional societies. It was institutionalised as an integral part of the Mandinke way of life centuries ago. And it preceded Islam.

Therefore the introduction of Islam to Africa has nothing to do with polygamy, or polygyny, in terms of establishing it on the continent. It just happens that it's in accord with the teachings of Islam. It's therefore sanctioned on religious grounds provided the husband can take care of his wives and is fair to all, favouring none.

Under Islam, a man can have up to four wives, a precept that does not conflict with traditional Mandinka culture. But although polygamy is common, it's rare for the men to have more than three wives.

As in most traditional societies across Africa, women who bear children, especially boys, are seen as the most successful. It's common in many societies across the continent to divorce their wives if they can't have children, oblivious of the fact that it's the husbands who may not be able to have children. Unfortunately, all the blame is placed on women.

In Mandinka culture, the senior wife, who is the first wife, has jurisdiction over the other wives. They're ranked in seniority, the last to be married being the most junior in rank regardless of her age.

Division of labour based on gender is enshrined in the traditional way of life among the Mandinka.

Men clear and till the land. They also plant groundnuts which is the the main cash crop not only for the Mandinka but for the vast majority of other Gambians and for the country as a whole. Groundnuts are also a major part of the Mandinka diet.

The men also plant other crops including maize and millet.

While groundnuts are a commercial commodity, even though some are for local consumption, other food crops such as millet and maize are mostly consumed locally.

Women also work on the farms. But they specialise in taking care of the rice fields.

Inheritance is patrilineal. Some women object to that but few challenge it because of cultural constraints.

Although the Mandinka are a separate ethnic group in The Gambia, they belong to a larger ethno-linguistic family, the Mande, which includes all the Mandinka – or Mandingo – tribes in other West African countries, including Chad in Central Africa.

Other groups which belong to the Mande family include the Bambara, the Bissa, the Bozo, and the Dyula. They are all Mandingo or Mandinka or Malinke, or sub-tribes of the larger Mandingo ethnic group, only with different names and sometimes different practices which give them their own identities as separate tribes.

But they're basically the same people, a situation somewhat analogous to the Ashanti and the Fanti in Ghana, the Zulu and the Ngoni in South Africa, the

Kikuyu and the Embu in Kenya, and so on. They also speak related languages.

Yet, they have their own separate identities as ethno-cultural entities even if they're considered to be sub-groups of a larger group or groups.

With regard to the Mandinka and related groups, Professor David C. Conrad of the History Department at the State University of New York, Oswego, New York, and Djanka Tassey Condé, state the following in their book *Sunjata: A West African Epic of the Mande Peoples*:

"Today historians and linguists have identified the closest living languages descended from those spoken at the royal court of the Mali Empire. These constitute a branch of the Mande language family referred to as 'Manding.'

This Manding group includes important languages such as Maninka (Fr. Malinke), Bamana (Fr. Bambara), Dyula, and Mandinka. These Manding languages have a high degree of interintelligibility, and some scholars prefer to characterize them as dialects or regional variations of a single language.

The Manding branch forms a continuum, with its epicenter in 'Manden,' the name given to the heartland of the old Mali Empire, and radiates outward from Mali and Guinea as far as Senegal in the west and Ivory Coast to the southeast.

There are perhaps as many as 20 million speakers of Manding languages, with about half of that number speaking a Manding language as a first language.

For linguists, the entire taxonomy of Mande languages in West Africa is based on levels of genetic interconnectedness to the core Mande languages known as 'Manding.'

In West Africa the names of ethnic groups and languages are often the same. For example, one can be a Mandinka and speak Mandinka, or be a Wolof and speak

Wolof – a non-Mande language. It is also possible for a Mandinka to speak Wolof, just as an Englishman might speak French.

Scholars speak of a 'Mandinka people' just as they refer to a 'Mandinka language.' Likewise, scholars have found it useful to talk of 'Manding peoples' – like the Mandinka or the Dyula – as a cultural subset of Mande language-speaking peoples, in the same way that 'Manding languages' are a branch of a much larger Mande language family.

It must be stressed, however, that there is no specific Mande or Manding *language*, but instead Mande and Manding *languages*.

In the same way, we cannot talk of the Mande or Manding *people*, but rather Mande and Manding *peoples* (emphasis by the authors in the original text, not by me – Godfrey Mwakikagile)." – (David C. Conrad and Djanka Tassey Condé, *Sunjata: A West African Epic of the Mande Peoples*, Indianapolis, Indiana, USA: Hackett Publishing Company, Inc., 2004, pp. xxxiii – xxxiv).

In addition to their transnational identity, the Mandinka also have a proud history as the descendants of the founders of the great Mali Empire which encompassed a vast expanse of territory which includes the areas of several countries in West Africa today.

One of its most prominent leaders was Sundiata Keita. He was the founder of the Mali Empire.

The Mandinka in The Gambia also have a unique distinction among all the Mandinka – or Malinke or Mandingo – groups. That's the only country where they constitute the largest ethnic group. In the rest of the countries, they're a minority.

Like their brethren in other countries in West Africa and in Chad in Central Africa, they live in compounds which comprise related members. The compounds collectively constitute a village. Therefore, a village in

Mandinka's traditional society is a community of related members.

That's the not the case with all the tribes in West Africa or in other parts of the continent.

Also, the majority of them don't have a high level of literacy in terms of what's described as Western education since it was brought to Africa by Europeans. But the majority of them can read Arabic even if they can not speak it fluently. Their knowledge of Arabic comes from studying the Quran in Quranic schools, a common practice in all the countries where Islam is practised.

They also acquire indigenous knowledge, as a form of education, from an early age. Boys are taught by their fathers, and girls by their mothers, responsibilities to their families and to their communities.

This kind of education is acquired from practice by using the skills they have been taught. The learning process in the traditional context also includes proverbs, which are nuggets of wisdom accumulated through the ages; it also includes songs and stories.

So, while it may be true that the majority – as in other tribes – don't have Western or modern education, they are not ignorant. They have the wisdom and practical skills they need to be effective members of their traditional societies.

It's the kind of education they need to be productive members of those societies. Any other kind of education they can't use is meaningless.

But there is also a need to acquire what's called modern education because it can also be used in traditional societies to make life easier and better.

The oral tradition play a very important role in Mandinka culture. In the absence of the written word, it's the repository of knowledge. It's also used to transmit knowledge from one generation to the next. And it has been used for centuries.

Griots are central to the Mandinka oral tradition as

reservouirs of knowledge and history of the Mandinka society. And the role they play is one of the most prominent features of the Mandinka traditional society; so is the musical instrument, the *kora*, which is virtually synonymous with Mandinka identity.

The *kora* is played when the griot is narrating oral history, singing praise, telling stories or playing any of the other roles he's traditionally assigned to play. Or it can be played simply as a musical instrument even when there's no griot performing his duties.

The role of the griot, who is also known as the jali, has been described in the following terms by some Gambians in their book *Sunjata: Gambian Versions of the Mande Epic*:

"In pre-colonial days, it was the freeborn who were the patrons of jalis. A particular family of jalis would remain for generations with a freeborn family, and thus they acquired detailed knowledge of the genealogies and family histories of their patrons.

One of the main functions of jalis is to sing or recite family histories and lineages on ritual occasions, and the story of Sunjata is an example of this type of recitation.

Part of this verbal art consists of reciting the 'praise names' of a family – with extensive use of obscure epithets such as 'cats on the shoulder,' not always directly understood, but often representing some episode from an important moment in the family history.

These name have the effect of heightening the emotional tension of a narrative – without necessarily advancing the story – and Mande listeners who are praised in this way by a skilled jali will often reward them generously.

The jali has many other important ritual and social functions. He or she acts as a go-between during disputes, as confidential adviser on many matters ranging from business to marriage, and as a public spokesperson. For example, it is still uncommon in the Gambia today for a local chief or other dignitary to raise his or her voice at a public meeting. Instead, the message will be passed in low tones to a jali, who will then proclaim the announcement, often embellishing the original words....

Although colonialism has undermined traditional systems of kinship, jalis continue to fulfil an important social role in contemporary Mande society, throughout the Mande diaspora.

Virtually any ceremonial or festive occasion requires the presence of a jali: their music is the ubiquitous backdrop to weddings, child-naming parties, religious festivities, national holidays, even political rallies.

Their praise songs in memory of former kings and warriors – often adapted to honour leading members of contemporary society such as businessmen men and politicians – fill the airwaves of radio and television stations.

The most famous of these jalis, especially in Mali and Guinea, sometimes receive gifts from their patrons of extraordinary generosity: money, houses, cars, land, even, in the case of one female singer, a small airplane.

They are symbols of traditional Mande values in the modern world....

A Sunjata tune, one that is sung to proclaim his bravery – 'Death is better then disgrace' – was adopted as the Mali national anthem....

Thus the Sunjata story circulates widely in many guises.

Full-length epic recitations, however, are now rare. They tend to be reserved for special, ceremonial occasions such as the re-roofing of the sacred hut (*kamablon*) in Kangaba (Mali), and only certain jalis are authorized to participate in the performance.

To our knowledge, no such ritual or commemorative occasions exist in the Gambia, being far away from the Mande heartland. Instead, the most likely contexts in which a long version of Sunjata might be recited are the *sumungolu*. These are private informal gatherings held in the evening at a patron's house, in which the jali sits and recites stories, with musical accompaniment, for the patron's edification and entertainment.

The atmosphere at such gatherings can be highly charged, with frequent interruptions and excited exclamations of 'It's true!,' as the jali evokes the great heroes of the past through song." – (*Sunjata: Gambian Versions of The Mande Epic*, op.cit., pp. xvi – xvi, xviii).

Also central to the Mandinka way of life is the rite of passage. The practice starts at an early age preparing the young for adulthood as responsible members of society. It involves both boys and girls.

Apart from learning social responsibilities they are required to fulfill when they're growing up as responsible members of their communities, they're also taught the significance of their identity as Mandinka; how important it is to be a Mandinka, and what it means to be Mandinka. They're also taught rules of behaviour including the way they should behave before older people; how they should relate to their peers; how they should treat members of the opposite sex and other members of society.

The training is done by older people of the same sex who become very important in the lives of the youths to whom they're imparting knowledge. They end up having a lasting relationship throughout their lives, establishing special bonds which help to strengthen the community to which they all belong.

Inextricably linked with all this is religion. Success in life, whether one adheres to the teachings of the elders or not, is also determined by forces beyond one's control. And that's when religion, including traditional beliefs, come into play. Most Mandinkas who have embraced Islam also practise traditional beliefs.

The most important figure in all this is the marabout

who can do good or evil on behalf of the individual seeking his help.

Marabouts invoke the Quran when performing their duties. And they give their clients talismans or amulets for protection.

Hidden inside the protective amulets the people wear to ward off evil or attract luck are verses from the Quran copied and written on a piece of paper by the marabout. Even many highly educated people believe in the power of these protective amulets and talismans. As stated in *Sunjata: Gambian Versions of The Mande Epic*:

"Parts of the Mande world, especially near the heartland, have been Islamic since the time of Sunjata. The Mandinka, however, were among the last group of Mande to be converted to Islam, a process which did not fully take place until the end of the 19th century.

Their practice of Islam therefore retains many aspects of pre-Islamic belief in esoteric power, and this is amply reflected in the two Sunjata texts in this book.

Thus, we find in these narratives that the religious clerics, locally known as marabouts, are continually called upon by both Sunjata and Susu Sumanguru to fabricate power-objects such as amulets, as well as to engage in various forms of divination." – (*Sunjata: Gambian Versions of The Mande Epic*, op.cit., p. xvii).

Some Christians in the Mandinka tribe – and in other ethnic groups – also practise traditional religious beliefs, incorporating them into their Christian faith. But they're also an anomaly in a predominantly Muslim society. Some of them have even been isolated or rejected by their Muslim families for embracing Christianity.

But in spite of all that, the country remains tolerant of diverse religious beliefs even if there are cases of intolerance by a number of individuals here and there. Religious intolerance is not an omnipresent phenomenon in The Gambia.

Still, with the exception of Gambia's Creole, the Aku, all ethnic groups have been strongly influenced by Islam not only in terms of worship but also in the way they live. Even their languages have been influenced by Islam. The Mandinka are no exception. According to a work edited by Anders Pettersson, *Literary History: Towards A Global Perspective:Notions of Literature Across Times and Cultures*:

"Many Islamic elements have been culturally transposed and integrated into the Mandinka people's language, orature and daily life.

These originally Islamic categories live their own lives as naturalized parts of the Mandinkas' world. Obvious and well known, the Mandinka consider them integral to their own culture and even use them as expressions of their cultural identity." – (Anders Pettersson, ed., *Literary History: Towards A Global Perspective:Notions of Literature Across times and Cultures, Vol. 1*, Berlin, Germany: Walter de Gruyter GmbH & Co., 2006, p. 287).

Their culture is Malinke in essence, hence African in origin, in spite of the foreign elements – including Islam – which it has incorporated.

It's a dynamic and resilient culture. And it's highly productive across the spectrum and has been that way for centuries.

The Mandinka or Mandingo or Malinke have also produced some of the most well-known African leaders in modern times. They include Sekou Toure who was the first president of Guinea, and Modibo Keita, the first president of Mali. And so is Jawara, of course, the first president of The Gambia.

All these Mandingo leaders spearheaded the independence struggle in their respective countries. And the history of their people is inextricably linked with colonial history, as demonstrated in the case of The Gambia. As Professor Paulla A. Ebron of the Anthropology Department at Stanford University states in her book *Performing Africa*:

"In The Gambia, Mandinka culture and history has seemed by far the most suitable...for a nation-making heritage.
Mandinka constitute the largest ethnic group in The Gambia. Under British authority, Mandinka chiefs residing primarily in the Upper-River division of the country formed the backbone of the system of indirect rule. Mandinka culture became the unmarked 'native' culture of colonial discourse in The Gambia.
At independence, important Mandinka families maintained political prominence. Furthermore, Mandinka had the heritage of kingdoms that could allow the nation to imagine a politically powerful past and future. They were not merely a circumscribed ethnic group; they were the descendants of kings.
The heritage of kingdoms allowed national historians the possibilities of imagining once and future political power and independence. It allowed a sense of the kind of political relationships that might productively order an independent and active political space.
Culture as custom simply orders everyday life; culture as imperial heritage makes possible a politically powerful present and future." – Paulla A. Ebron, *Performing Africa*, Princeton University Press, 2002, p. 90).

Culture also reinforces an already existing identity and helps to construct a new one in a larger national context by invoking a glorious past and even a not-so-glorious past.
And for a once-colonised people, as we once were in Africa, invocation of culture is a re-affirmation of our very being, essence, and existence as an independent people before the advent of colonial rule.

We reclaimed our independence on attainment of sovereign status following the end of colonial rule under which we had been subjugated.

The reclamation of our independence was a natural right. As one African philosopher, Dr. Willie E. Abraham from Ghana, put it, independence is a state of nature. It's a sentiment that still echoes across the continent. See, for example, Godfrey Mwakikagile, *Africa and The West*:

"The democratic way of life in our traditional society was profoundly affected when Europeans imposed alien rule on us.

From then on, the colonialists had the final say in the conduct of our affairs. And our struggle for independence was rooted in this very idea of democracy as a natural right we had enjoyed for centuries before the advent of colonial rule, and in the universal belief that we were entitled to freedom just like everybody else. As one African philosopher put it, independence is a state of nature – and one to be 'gained' only because it had been lost, certainly not as something new.[77]

Therefore even after we were subdued by imperial might, there was always the hope that, in spite of all the odds against us given the technological superiority of our conquerors, one day, somehow by every means at our disposal, we would regain that independence.

And there is abundant evidence across the continent that Africans never gave up." – (Godfrey Mwakikagile, *Africa and The West*, Huntington, New York: Nova Science Publishers, Inc., 2000, pp. 33 – 35. See also Willie E. Abraham, *The Mind of Africa*, London: Weidenfeld & Nicolson, 1967, p. 152; and Ali A. Mazrui, *Towards A Pax Africana: A Study of Ideology and Ambition*, London: Weidenfeld & Nicolson, 1967, p. 250).

As the founders of one of the most successful independent nations in Africa, the Mali Empire which was really a macro-nation, the Mandinka or Mandingo were one of the most proud symbols of African independence and dignity before the coming of Europeans.

And the Mandinka culture even today in The Gambia – and in other parts of West Africa – is just one example of Africa's glorious past, and one of the best in terms of achievements before the invasion of our continent by foreigners.

After the Mandinka, we're going to look at the Fula next, the second-largest ethno-cultural group in The Gambia.

The Fula

The Fula – or Fulani or Fulbe or Peul – are one of the most prominent ethnic groups in the entire West Africa, not just in The Gambia.

They're found in many countries in West Africa. Some also live in western Sudan. They constitute a minority in all those countries except Guinea where they're the largest group, making up 40 per cent of the total population.

In spite of their minority status in most of the countries in which they live, they have been highly influential in the region for centuries. In Nigeria, for example, they have together with their allies the Hausa dominated the government since independence.

They have been rulers in different parts of West Africa, a dominance that's also partly responsible for the creation of a caste system in their society and in the societies they have ruled.

Their rise to prominence in spite of their numerical inferiority in the region is as fascinating as it's intriguing; so is their history. According to an article, "History Corner – Peoples of The Gambia: The Fula," in one of Gambia's leading newspapers, the *Daily Observer*:

"Various versions have been given by historians about

the origins of the Fula.

One version is that they were originally a Berber-speaking people who crossed the Senegal to pasture their cattle on the Ferlo Plateau.

Finding themselves cut off from their kinsmen by the Negroid communities occupying the fertile Senegal valley, they gradually adopted the language of their new neighbours.

As their herds increased, small groups found themselves forced to move eastward and so initiated a series of migrations throughout West Africa.

Another main version given about the origins of the Fula is that they originated in the lower basins of the Senegal and The Gambia as a result of a mixture between Berbers from the Sahara and the Wollof and Serer peoples.

This view is held because, among other things, the Fulani language is akin to the languages of these peoples. The union between Berber, Wollof and Serer was said to produce two distinct groups of Fulani with differences in racial and occupational characteristics.

One of the groups, the predominantly Berber portion, marked by their olive skin and straight hair, stuck to the nomadic mode of life and became known as the Bororoje or Cattle Fulani.

The other group of Fulani, known as the Fulani Gidda, was the Negroid portion who were agriculturalist and town dwellers for the most part.

Whatever explanation is accepted about the origins of the Fula, it is known that by at least the seventh century, the Fula were a distinct people in the Western Sudan and among the first West Africans to embrace Islam.

Fula society was also a stratified society of three main social groups. At the top of the social ladder were the Rimbe who were free men and included farmers and traders.

Next to the Rimbe came the Nyenyube who formed the artisan class and finally the Machudo who were the servant class.

The Nyenyube class included the Gaulo or praise signgers, the Bailo who were the smith, the Garanke or leather workers and the Laube who were weavers.

The Gaulo were oral historians who played the important role of preserving Fula traditions and culture.

The Fulas who first migrated into The Gambia area were non-Muslim pastoralists who came to ask for protection from the Mandinka Mansas into whose states they brought their cattle.

They lived in small communities in the chief Mandinka towns and cared for the herds and flocks of the Mansas in return for projection against attacks from hostile groups.

Nine dialects have been identified, reflecting different areas of origin, period of arrival and considerable cultural diversity. This diversity seems to have dissipated the political impact of their numbers.

In the nineteenth century, the main Fula settlements were in the kingdoms of the upper river: Wuli, Niani, Kantora, Tomana and Jimara.

Generally, the Fula migrants acknowledged the authority of the Mandinka Mansas and village chiefs over the use of land. A mutually beneficial relationship existed between them and the Mandinka leaders. In return for the protection afforded the Fulas by the Mandinka Mansas, the Fula brought wealth and prestige to those communities they settled in.

In their spread throughout West Africa, the Fula founded states called 'Imamates.'

The Imamate was a new kind of state in West Africa where the head of state was also the Imam and leader of the mosque.

Futa Jallow was the first of these Imamates. The 'Al-mamy,' who ruled the state, was very powerful and claimed to rule in the name of Allah, but had to listen to the advice of his counsellors.

The Al-mamy was the military commander of his state

heading an army that was based on a strict system of compulsory service.

One of the most remarkable examples of the dispersal of peoples in West Africa is afforded by the Fulani.

Today some of the best cattle attendants in West Africa are the Fulani and are to be found in almost every part of the Savannah-Sahel region from The Gambia to Sudan.

The Fulani began their migrations into the regions of Ghana, Manding and Songhai between the twelfth and sixteenth centuries, entering Hausaland in the fifteenth century.

In all these areas, they maintained their traditional way of life, the Bororoje sticking to the rural areas, and the Fulani Gidda to the towns.

Because of their literacy in Arabic, the Fulani Gidda were employed in Hausaland as civil servants, diplomats, and tutors at the courts of the Hausa kings, while some of them established schools of their own and taught Islamic theology, law and Arabic grammar.

One of these Fulani Gidda was Ousman Dan Fodio who was born in 1754 in Hausaland but whose ancestral family had migrated to the area from Futa Toro some fourteen generations before.

Places like Bauchi and Adamawa became converted to Islam for the first time.

If today Islam is a force to reckon with in Nigeria, and in deed in the modern states of The Gambia, Senegal, Mali, Guinea, and Niger, it was because of the Fula-led revolutionary Islamic movements of the late eighteenth and nineteenth centuries, in general, and that of Ousman Dan Fodio in particular." – ("History Corner – Peoples of The Gambia: The Fula," in the *Daily Observer*, Banjul, The Gambia, 5 February 2008).

Usman Dan Fodio established a Fulani dynasty in northern Nigeria, dominating the entire region, and is one of the most prominent Fulanis in history. Other prominent

Fulanis include Nigeria's first prime minister Abubakar Tafawa Balewa; and the first president of Cameroon, Ahmadou Ahidjo.

One of they ways which has enabled the Fulani to spread their influence in many parts of West Africa is their nomadic lifestyle.

This lifestyle has also influenced their language through the years. Many words from the languages of the people they have intermingled with have been incorporated into the Fulani language.

The Fulani were among the first people in West Africa to convert to Islam. And they played a major role in spreading the religion through Jihad, facilitated by their nomadic lifestyle and by trade.

So three factors were responsible for the spread of Fulani influence in West Africa: Islam, nomadic lifestyle, and trade in which the Fulani have been engaged for a long time. They're some of the most prominent traders in West Africa.

Nigeria provides one of the best examples of Fulani influence and power, which is an integral part of their culture, in that region of West Africa. As stated in a book edited by Professor Maghan Keita of the History Department at Villanova University, *Conceptualizing/Re-Conceptualizing Africa: The Construction of African Historical Identity*:

"Though the Jihad had been conceived in a spirit of egalitarianism, and drew its support from a socially diverse population, its leadership had been primarily Fulani.

The Fulani became the primary beneficiaries of the emirate system. In fact, with the exception of Yakubu of Bauchi, all of the emirs were Fulani, though some *Habe* – non-Fulfulde speaking – leaders, like Abd al-Salam, were also given high positions in the new administration (Johnson 1967).

This new Fulani ruling elite controlled the wealth producing military functions – the procuring of booty and slaves – which reinforced the new system of social stratification.

Fulani ethnicity which, though present, had not been politically important prior to the Jihad, began to define political relationships in the nineteenth century.

Greater power and higher status accrued to Fulani clan leaders who consolidated their control through intermarriage and clientship; office holding became associated with religious knowledge, ties to the Jihad, and kinship (Hendrixson 1981).

The Fulani restated the traditional stratification system in ethnic terms; ruling was identified with the Fulani.

However, the complexity of this system of social stratification should not be underestimated. Certainly there was a Fulani aristocracy, but the relationship between the Fulani, *as an ethnic group*, and the rest of the population, was often ambiguous.

Through interaction, intermarriage and the subsequent assimilation of the non-Muslim, nomadic Fulani into the multi-ethnic, sedentary society of Kasar Hausa, geography and occupational specialization retained their considerable importance as foci of identification.

The Caliphate was still an ethnically heterogeneous polity in which being 'Hausa' was not the critical variable which separated the talakawa from the emerging *Fulbe* – Fulfulde speaking – aristocracy; nor does it follow that because Islam provided the ideological justification that united this vast empire, that it was conterminous with a 'Hausa-Fulani' ethnic group prior to the British conquest at the turn of the century." – (Maghan Keita, editor, *Conceptualizing/Re-Conceptualizing Africa: The Construction of African Historical Identity*, Boston, Massachusetts, USA: Brill Academic Publishers, 2002, pp. 21 – 22).

The complexity of this social stratification which was not exclusively Fulani in terms of demographic composition is illuminated further in this context:

"If we turn to Katsina in the second half of the nineteenth century, we can see that the complex political, social, and economic relationships in the emirates of the Sokoto Caliphate can not be reduced to simply Fulani ruling over Hausa.

For example, in the reign of Emir Ibrahim (1871 – 1883) there were three main sections of the central administration in Katsina, which were called *bayin sarki* (lit: slaves of the emir). They were responsible for conducting the official business of the palace, the treasury, and the army directly under the emir; they also collected taxes throughout the emirate.

Besides being the primary executive arm of the emir, the *bayan sarki* provided many of the officials responsible for regulating and supervising specialized economic activities such as weaving, dyeing, tanning, woodcarving, building, salt trading, market and caravan organization, butchering, and the cultivation of various food products.

The *bayan sarki* formed a distinct social strata (sic) of heterogeneous origin, but with a corporate identity and outlook. Moreover, some of the *bayan sarki* had lineage affiliations which could be traced to the pre-jihad government, while others were recruited from groups which had moved into Katsina more recently (Usman 1981).

This phenomenon was not unique to Katsina. We see an ethnically heterogeneous ruling structure emerging in many of the emirates in the second half of the nineteenth century. For example, although detailed information about every state is not immediately accessible, there is evidence to suggest the prominence, if not the predominance, of slave officials in late nineteenth century Jam'are, Adamawa, Nupe, and Ilorin (Smaldone 1977).

Indeed, during the second half of the nineteenth century, the ascendancy of slave officials of various ethnic backgrounds, especially as military commanders, seems to have been universal throughout the Sokoto Caliphate. Furthermore, during this period, the power of ethnically heterogeneous palace slaves, equipped with firearms, was increased in the emirates, and that of the Fulani *hakamai* was circumscribed." – (Ibid., pp. 22 – 23).

The Fula who settled in The Gambia did not rise to prominence as the rulers of the area the way their brethren did in Nigeria and in other parts of West Africa. But they have, nevertheless, played an important role through the years in shaping the country's cultural landscape as much as their brethren have elsewhere only in varying degrees of success.

The Fula in The Gambia migrated from Senegal, Guinea and Mali. And they established themselves in the Upper River area of Gambia in the 1800s.

Their society is structured on the basis of family units, the clan, ancestral ties of lineal descendants, and the ethnic group itself.

Although some of them intermarried with the members of other tribes such as the Wolof and the Mandinka, they remained Fula in terms of culture. They were determined to preserve their customs and values to perpetuate their identity and heritage.

This attitude also played a major role in the way they structured their society, leading to the establishment of a caste system.

Their caste system still exists today. It's divided into four castes: there is the noble class which includes the rulers and other powerful people; traders; blacksmiths; and the descendants of slaves.

Slaves constituted the lowest class. But they were a very important part of the Fulani traditional society.

Slaves were also sometimes accepted as members of

the family; and when they were, they took the names of their masters; a situation similar to what happened in the United States where African slaves became "Jackson," "Smith," "Patterson," "Johnson," "Williams," "Watson," and so on, taking their slave masters' last names, mostly British.

Although their nomadic lifestyle has taken them to different parts of West Africa – grazing their cattle, sheep and goats – where they have also settled, they have also maintained their culture partly by living separately from other groups. They have a tendency to stick with their own kind.

They also tend to marry within their own group. They even marry their own cousins, a taboo in many traditional societies across Africa.

Yet, in spite of their strong sense of group identity, they have intermarried with the members of other ethnic groups in the areas where they have settled.

And as in many other ethnic groups in different parts of Africa, arranged marriages are still common among the Fulani; so is polygyny. It's common for a Fula man to have two wives.

Unmarried men are rare among them. Every man is expected to get married sometime in his life even if he stays single for a very long time. Divorce is rare.

Their ability to forge ties with other groups in spite of their strong group identity has enabled them to spread their influence over extensive areas far beyond their numbers. And there is no question that they played a major role in establishing a network of trade routes throughout much of West Africa, along which they also spread Islam and gained influence and eventually leadership over other groups in the region through the years.

Their physical appearance, together with the way they dress, also distinguishes them from the members of other ethnic groups.

They also have other distinctive cultural characteristics

which make them stand out among other groups around them. For example, one of the most distinguishing characteristics of Fula women is their tendency to use henna to blacken their lips, besides their preference for necklaces, earrings and anklets among other items.

And although they're basically the same people, they're also divided by language. Their language, Fulfulde, has 11 dialects spoken in different parts of West Africa, reinforced by regional differences and separation through the years.

Their lifestyle has also changed through the years. They're basically a nomadic people in terms of culture and history. But as whole, non-nomadic Fulanis now outnumber their nomadic brethren throughout West Africa; a fundamental change which has had a profound impact on their demographic pattern in terms of where they live. Some are semi-nomadic, their lifestyle dictated by seasonal changes.

Among Fula pastoralists, some women milk cows and take care of the livestock. That's in sharp contrast with what goes on in many other traditional societies where men milk the cows and tend livestock. For example, in my tribe, the Nyakyusa, women don't milk cows; men do.

But the practice – of women milking cows – is not widespread even among the Fulani, a fact documented by a number of researchers including Professor Lucy E. Creevey of the University of Connecticut who specialises in comparative politics and women in political development – among other areas – in her book, *Women Farmers in Africa: Rural Development in Mali and the Sahel*:

"Our methodology involved systematic observation of village women in their daily routines, interviews with women on selected livestock-related topics, meetings held with groups of women to ascertain their opinions concerning livestock practices, and development and administration of a questionnaire which was given to seventy-one women concerning their current livestock practices and their attitudes about possible women's roles in the development of the livestock sector....

Young women go on transhumance with their husbands, but in general are not responsible for herding cattle or taking them to waterholes. However, women sometimes go ahead, to look for new pastures. Vaccinations and other medications for animals arc usually paid for by the men in whose herds the animals graze.

The importance of cattle to Fulani women lies particularly in the milk they produce. All of the women who were interviewed milked cows. As women enter their husbands' households, they are allocated cows for milking purposes. Women may also milk cattle belonging to their children, as long as the animals remain in the family herd and are not redistributed to the son's wife or removed by a daughter to her husband's herds.

All of the Fulani women we interviewed reserve part of each day's milk supply for their family's use. However, in the rainy season, when there is a good supply of milk, more milk is sold than is kept in the household. As the dry season progresses, cows produce less milk, and in January a woman may obtain only one liter from three cows, compared with six liters during the rainy season (Henderson 1980: 123). When there is sufficient milk supply, Fulani women also make soap, butter, and yogurt – (Lucy E. Creevey, *Women Farmers in Africa: Rural Development in Mali and the Sahel*, Syracuse, New York: Syracuse University Press, First Edition, 1986, pp. 134, and 138).

So, among the Fulani, men still play a major role in taking care of livestock even when women milk cows. They also move from place to place with their cows in search of water and pasture during the dry season. This is especially done by younger men. As Mohammed Toure, chairman of the Great Fulani Association in Accra, Ghana – about whom more later – put it: "We follow our cow...and forget our home."

Semi-nomadic Fulanis return to their villages with their livestock during the wet season. During this period, some women also milk the cows.

Gender roles are well-defined; so is distribution of power.

Structured as a hierarchy, Fulani society is highly competitive, an attribute that has contributed substantially to the rise of the Fulani to power in many parts of West Africa during their history.

But such dominance has also led to conflict with other groups who resent Fulani domination.

Some of them also accuse the Fulani of being prejudiced against other groups whom they consider to be inferior to them. And the fact that typical Fulanis – with a light complexion, straight or wavy hair, pointed nose, thin lips and other "Caucasian" features – even look different from the members of other African ethnic groups who have dark skin, "kinky" hair, "wide" noses, "wide" faces, "big" lips, and short necks, only makes things worse.

The Fulani have a rigid code of conduct among themselves and for their children. And as in most societies across Africa, the process of socialisation and initiation into society starts early. Boys learn from their fathers and other men; girls from their mothers and other women especially relatives. They know where they belong, what they're expected to do, and when.

This knowledge of self and of their society not only reinforces their Fulani identity and prepares them for adulthood; it also prepares them for marriage. They know whom they're supposed to marry. And they know which social class they belong to. Arranged marriages are between social equals. They not only know what class they belong to; they know not to cross the line.

The mobility of the Fulani also has had an impact on

their lifestyle and has even reshaped their identity in some cases in different regional contexts. These changes have taken place because of the imperative need for survival which has compelled many Fulanis – or Fulas – to move from place to place, live in different social settings, and engage in different social and economic activities.

And in spite of the different experiences they have undergone in different countries and societies, the essence of Fula identity remains the same. It's transnational, forming a common bond among all Fulanis even when they really have different identities which have been shaped by different historical circumstances.

This common Fulani identity, in spite of their different national identities, was defined by one Fulani leader, Mohammed Toure, chairman of the Great Fulani Association in the Greater Accra area in Ghana in transnational terms which may help shed some light on how the Fulani see themselves beyond their national confines – whether they are in The Gambia, Ghana, Guinea, Mali or anywhere else. As Ghanaian Professor Yaa P. A. Oppong of Harvard University states in her book *Moving Through and Passing On: Fulani Mobility, Survival, and Identity in Ghana*:

"In February 1997, the end of the Muslim fasting period of Ramadan was celebrated by the Muslim people of Nima, Accra, with a procession through the main street. There were over a dozen different associations taking part in the parade, many of which had formed on the basis of ethnic group affiliation.

The Fulani procession was organized by the Great Fulani Association, a *suudu-baaba* that was known throughout the Fulani community in Greater Accra. This particular organization was established by Ghanaian-born Fulani.

The women in the Fulani procession had their hair intricately plaited and were carrying large calabashes of fresh milk on their heads. The men were dressed as herdsmen. The costumes they were wearing, traditional Nigerian Fulani dress, had been chosen by elder members of the association.

'You see, the Mali[an] dress is different. The Burkina ones are also different, Niger also has different traditional dress. This year it was the Nigerian Fulani dress that we chose. Last year we used the Burkina Fulani dress. God willing next year we will choose a different dress, maybe we will choose Cameroon or Mali, or Gambia or other countries.' – (Mohammed Toure, Chairman of the Great Fulani Association)....

Inherent in the decision to choose a Fulani costume from one of the various West African countries was the acknowledgement that there is no Ghanaian Fulani dress and that way the way Fulani dress and present themselves varies enormously from country to country. In other words, Fulani may be *in* Ghana but they are not *of* Ghana in the sense that they have no traditions and way of dressing unique to them." – (Yaa P. A. Oppong, *Moving Through and Passing On: Fulani Mobility, Survival, and Identity in Ghana*, New Brunswick, New Jersey, USA: Transaction Publishers, 2002, pp. 1 – 2).

The procession was also a celebration of Fulani diversity and of Ghana's diversity. The celebration also had religious symbolism as a unity of Muslims.

But it was mainly an acknowledgement of Fulani common identity, embracing all Fulanis – including the Fula in The Gambia – in spite of the diversity amongst them. Therefore the message was also a universal one and very clear: "We are all Fulani." As Mohammed Toure explained:

"The ladies and young men, we made them one dress so that when you saw them you would know that it was the Fulani who were coming. Did you see us drinking milk in the streets?....now we know that we have gone home, we are in Ghana but we remember home." – (Mohammed Toure, ibid., p. 2).

The Fula in The Gambia would have equally felt at home among their brethren in Ghana and at that event celebrating common Fulani identity. As Oppong states in her book:

"This public celebration of Fulani identity on the streets of Accra illustrates the many identities of the Fulani. Here, in this very public arena, were members of the Fulani community – many of whom were, as the vice president (of the Great Fulani Association) put it in a common phrase, 'made in Ghana' – celebrating the diversity of Fulani experience in West Africa on the one hand and on the other proclaiming that they were 'unified' and 'one' in Ghana.
Here were the Fulani processing alongside the Wangara, Kado, Zabarama, the Niger Youth Association, groups that were Muslim but were not of Ghanaian origin, as well as Northern Ghanaian ethnic groups such as the Dagomba.
Their relationship with other Muslim, 'northern,' peoples was being expressed and celebrated.
The street parade made visual many of the pertinent issues and problems involved in a discussion of Fulani identity, not least their geographical spread and attempts to foster unity among people of diverse origins." – (Yaa P. A. Oppong, *Moving Through and Passing On: Fulani Mobility, Survival, and Identity in Ghana*, ibid., p. 2).

What has been cited here in the Ghanaian context with regard to the Fulani is broadly representative of a group which comprises sub-groups with their own identities and their own characteristics.
There are many Fulani groups, including the ones

known as Fula in The Gambia. The identities of these Fulani sub-groups overlap with the identities of other groups within their respective regions, countries or localities with whom they interact. And this interaction has produced, shaped and reshaped the identities of the different Fulani groups because of the interactions which have taken place with their neighbours through the years and even centuries.

Therefore, although they are also Fulani, the Fula in The Gambia are different from their brethren in Nigeria, Mali, Guinea, Senegal, Sierra Leone, Ivory Coast, or in any of the other countries where they live because they have been shaped by different historical circumstances although they are, at the same time, essentially Fulani, mainly in terms of common origin more than anything else.

It's an identity that transcends national boundaries; an identity the Fulani in the diaspora and those at home are proud of. Yet, these same boundaries have also shaped their separate identities.

Mohammed Toure put it succinctly when different Fulani groups from different countries held a procession – of unity and solidarity – in the streets of Accra, Ghana, to celebrate their common identity when he said: "Now we know that we have gone home, we are in Ghana but we remember home."

The Gambia is home to one of the most prominent Fulani groups in West Africa who also constitute the second-largest ethnic entity in the country.

But ethnicity is an elastic concept, and probably even more so with regard to groups such as the Fulani who have undergone a lot of changes through the centuries from the time they came into existence as a distinct group.

Even their formation as an ethnic group involved many changes. They did not evolve or come into existence overnight. Their ethnic identity has also evolved through the years assuming many forms or even multiple identities under different circumstances, during different historical periods, and in different regions, also leading to the formation and evolution of many Fulani identities and not just one.

But whether these identities have been de-constructed and then reconstructed through the centuries or not to get where they are today, and to be what they are, the fact remains that there are such people who are known as the Fulani. Otherwise we would not even be talking about them. They do exist. And they do have an identity as a people and even different ethnic identities associated with, or which identify, different Fulani groups in different countries and regions, each with its own identity.

Yet their very existence as a people poses challenges. There are different Fulanis even in terms of physical appearance. Many of them don't have "typical" Fulani physical features which are sometimes described as Caucasian. They look just like any other black African with so-called typical "Negro" features – black skin, "kinky" or curly hair, "big" lips, "wide" nose, "short" neck, "flat" face, and so on – in sharp contrast with the Caucasian features of typical Fulanis.

And they *are* mostly black African, a product of typical black African tribes such as the Mandingo, with very little "Caucasian" – or Semitic – blood of the Fulani.

In fact, some of them don't even have any Fulani ancestry but identify themselves as Fulani because they were absorbed by the Fulani and became an integral part of Fulani society and Fulani ethnic identity.

Then there are those who say they're Fulani because they are ashamed of their black African – "Negro" – identity and don't want to identify themselves with their own people: black Africans who are members of typical black African tribes.

All this has led some people to challenge the assumptions underlying Fulani ethnic identity. They even question the existence and legitimacy of Fulani ethnic identity, contending there is no such thing. As Jean-Loup Amselle – director of Ecole des Hautes Etudes en Sciences Sociales (EHESS), a social science research institution in Paris, and editor of the *Journal of African Studies* – states in his book *Mestizo Ligics: Anthropology of Identity in Africa and Elsewhere*:

"The history of Fulani studies is a long disappointing pursuit of a chimera: the phenotype of a pure Fulani race that can be assigned to Fulani societies that existed historically....

Attempts to identify the pure Fulani race began as a long expedition in the nineteenth century with the physical anthropologists and the specialists of *Völkerkunde*. It continues to this day. Certain anthropologists freely include skull measurements in their data, or suggest a continuity between the herders depicted in the Saharan Tassili n'Ajer frescoes and the nomadic Fulani of West Africa today.

The pure, true Fulani is the red, nomadic Fulani, *Baddado* with nappy hair who considers himself white and who practices *pulaaku*, that is, the manner of conducting oneself as Fulani. This manner, a sort of Spinozist *conatus*, is characterized by resignation (*munyal*), intelligence (*hakkillo*), courage (*cuusal*), but especially discretion or reserve (*seemteende*). As M. Dupire has remarked, the first three values are found in many other African societies, but so is the last one as well.

These values characterize all aristocratic West African societies, whether sedentary or nomadic. They could in no way genuinely define anything unique to the Fulani.

If it is difficult to identify the Fulani by something other than the language, which has many dialects, the task becomes even more complicated when one considers seminomad or sedentary pagan Fulani living among blacks and speaking a language other than the one assigned to them....

The innumerable historical expressions of Fulani essence are perceived as so many cases of treason in relation to the model, because the identity of the group can be defined only in a system of relations involving neighboring identities.

The term Fulani *(Peul)* is itself ambiguous. According to Boilat, it should be Wolof. 'Fula,' which gave the fifteenth- and sixteenth-century Portuguese Foul, Fulos, or Fulas, is a Mandingo category according to Monteil, just as is the term *pullo* (plural *fulbe*)." – (Jean-Loup Amselle, *Mestizo Ligics: Anthropology of Identity in Africa and Elsewhere*, Stanford University Press, 1998, pp. 43, 44, 45).

He goes on to state:

"In analyzing the concepts and institutions that supposedly characterize the Fulani as an ethnic group, one finds numerous terms to be of Arabic origin or common to other languages in the region, such as the terms *satigi*, *saltigui*, or *siratik*, which designate the sovereigns of certain West African Fulani kingdoms.

At first glance, this expression, borrowed from the Mandingo language and meaning 'master of the road,' refers to the herders or tenders of the flocks, the traditional activity of Fulani chiefs.

But how accurate is it to see this as a borrowing?

Before asking if the Fulani have borrowed from the Mandingo or the Mandingo from the Fulani, we must first question the validity of any idea of borrowing that follows from a partition between Fulani and Mandingo.

What was just said regarding the notion of *satigi* can apply to many other Fulani cultural traits. Dupire notes that the eastern Fulani nomads fight with a Tuareg spear and that the *bori* cults of possession are also found among the Hausa.

These examples, to mention only a few, show what

several anthropologists have observed, namely, that one can become Fulani or Toucouleur, and that, inversely, the Fulani will convert ethnically to become Hausa or Bambara.

Rather than asking, for example, how the Fulani archetype – the Bodaado pagan practicing ritual flagellation (*soro*) – hybridizes to give rise to other avatars of the Fulani ethnic group: black, Islamized, city dwellers, and so on, it would be more appropriate to postulate a primary multiethnic situation that would include, for example, those people speaking the related languages of Fulani, Serer, Wolof, Mandingo, or the Volta languages. A primary multiethnic situation would have given rise to the different ethnic entities in the forms eventually fixed by colonial thought.

Of course, in the case of the Fulani as well as the Tuareg or the Nile-Hamites, it is much easier for ethnologists or essayists to give free rein to their fantasies since their subjects are for the most part nomadic herders of flocks and these have always excited the imagination of authors craving pseudo-historical narratives.

It is known since Khazanov's work, however, that nomadism guarantees neither autonomy nor purity. As he has shown in a broadly comparative study, nomadic societies function in an extensively heteronomous fashion and cannot be understood independently of the surrounding context.

In this respect, the Fulani nomads do not constitute a self-sufficient enclave or a prehistoric holdover any more than do the other herding peoples. Quite the opposite situation prevails.

They are result of a complex historical grouping that includes sedentary agricultural societies, long-distance trade, and political states.

What astonishes researchers is this rigid conception of a Fulani essence, given the ubiquity of the Fulani themselves, who, though sometimes part of peasant societies, define themselves at other times as empire builders." – (Ibid., pp. 45 – 46).

The people who are known as Fulani today would not be what they are had all those movements, including intermarriages, not taken place through the centuries. They're a product of historical forces.

Yet, at the core of this Fulani identity is the Fulani essence which still takes us back into history to find out whether or not such a people, in their "pure" state as a distinct biological category, really existed.

Were there really no such people – regardless of what they were known back then – as an ethnic and even as a racial category and with their own physical characteristics?

The answer is obviously, "Yes," since even today there are such people with their own distinctive features.

They themselves were probably a product of racial intermingling before they migrated to where they are today and intermingled with other groups, primarily black Africans, creating another category of people who today include Fulanis who look just like any other black African; those who look racially mixed; and also the so-called "pure" Fulani with "Caucasian" features – light complexion, straight hair, pointed noses, thin lips and so on.

But the debate continues. As Jean-Loup Amselle contends:

"Since the Fulani are a social production, it is impossible to assign a single referent to this ethnonym. In fact, as many meanings of the term Fulani exist as there are actual expressions of Fulani essence. These run from a tentative integration into a chain of sedentary societies for nomadic Fulani, to their disappearance as a semiautonomous ethnic group, and to their integration into the statutory network of a large state.

Contrary to the racial and ethnological perspective defended by a certain number of Fulani specialists, no Fulani substance exists that eventually gave rise to the different avatars of Fulani-ness by degenerating, and interbreeding with neighboring dark-skinned people.

As historical beings, the Fulani result from a double process of absorption and elimination, or of coming together and expulsion, which encapsulates a large part of West African history just as it does probably of many other cultural units.

It is all the more true, then, that the past of this subcontinent cannot be analyzed as the product of a confrontation between the Fulani and other populations. B. Barry has shown that, in the case of the Futa Jalon, for example, the *jihad* of 1725 – 50 cannot be understood in terms of a Fulani-Jallonke conflict, but rather as the constitution of of a class-structured society based on Islam, a movement in which the Mandingo marabouts actively participated.

An examination of Fulani history from any region, but specifically the history of the Wasolon, requires, then, a total reversal of perspective: the most ancient texts regarding the whole of the area under investigation need to be consulted. Of course, fifteenth- and sixteenth-century West African Fulani history is difficult to reconstruct because, except for the *Tarikh*, we possess only the meager sources left by the Portuguese. However slim, these sources, combined with information in the oral tradition, suffice to challenge an essentialist and substantialist vision of the Fulani.

The different accounts convey the impression of a primary mixing from the earliest beginnings, and this makes it absurd to even pose the question of Fulani identity." – (Ibid., pp. 46 – 47).

But Fulani people do exist even if their composition may raise a number of questions regarding their true identity.

As a biological category, they may not exist today as they did in the past, if there was indeed such a category. But as a social definition, the term "Fulani" today identifies a group of people who are called Fulani regardless of their ethnic and racial backgrounds, origins or identities.

And there are some elements which, in a cultural context, constitute the essence of Fulani identity.

But some of those elements may not be uniquely Fulani even though, in combination with other elements, they do identify the Fulani as a distinct ethnic category based on a social and not on a biological definition of what a Fulani is. As Kate R. Hampshire states in a work edited by Carol R. Ember and Melvin Ember, *Encyclopedia of Medical Anthropology: Health and Illness in the World's Cultures Topics - Volume 2*:

"The Fulani ethnic category is fluid and its boundaries are fuzzy (e.g. Burnham, 1996)....

The sense of identity – what it means to be Fulani, specifically *FulBe* – is strongly and explictly expressed in the concept of *Pulaaku*.

Pulaaku is principally about control and restraint, linked with a strong sense shame – *semteende*. This includes being in complete control of one's emotional and physical needs, and is often defined in opposition to assumed *RiimaaiBe* traits of lack of self-control.

Another important aspect of *pulaaku* is cattle-ownership.

Despite the essentialist nature of this Fulani discourse on their culture, it would be wrong to see *pulaaku* as being uniform, unchanging, and representing all Fulani behavior. Individual Fulani construct and interpret *pulaaku* variously at different times and under different circumstances (Burnham, 1996; De Bruijn & Van Dijk, 1995). This is important in understanding people's responses to illness."

– (Kate R. Hampshire in Carol R. Ember and Melvin Ember, *Encyclopedia of Medical Anthropology: Health and Illness in the World's Cultures Topics - Volume 2*, Springer; First Edition, 2003, p. 656, and 657).

All that may indeed be an integral part of Fulani identity which, together with other attributes, may indeed give the Fulani a distinct identity.

But it's also an interesting attribute of the Fulani. What's so interesting about it is that it's identified as "Fulani" while it's not unique to the Fulani.

The Fulani are not the only people in Africa – or in the world – who have those qualities. They're not the only people who are capable of exercising self-control. And they're not the only people who have a strong sense of shame.

You find all that among the Mandingo, the Ewe, the Ashanti, the Zulu, the Edo, the Ngoni, the Bemba, the Digo, the Zaramo, the Kwere, the Kerewe, the Nyamwezi, the Gogo, the Ndengereko, the Fanti, the Yoruba, the Igbo, the Tiv, the Ogoni, the Dogon, the Zanaki, the Kikuyu, the Krahn, the Bondei, the Nyaturu, the Chewa, the Bemba, the Bena, the Ndebele, the Zigua, the Nyakyusa, the Shona, the Haya, the Venda, the Kpelle, the Vai, the Lunda, the Maasai, the Manda, the Mende, the Kisi, the Kisii, the Makonde, the Susu, the Kinga, the Kru, the Kamba, the Hehe, the Luhya, the Luo, the Xhosa, the Chaga, the Bakongo, the Ovimbundu, the Temne, and so on. The list goes on and on.

So, it's hardly an attribute of ethnic identity in terms of being unique to the Fulani as it's implied in the preceding quotation. It does not specifically identify any group. Instead, it's shared by all ethnic groups and by members of all races in every country and on every continent on planet Earth.

The following example may serve to illustrate another aspect of Fulani identity for purposes of comparative analysis. As Professor John N. Paden, International Studies, at George Mason University, states in his book *Religion and Political Culture in Kano*:

"In practice, Hausa ethnicity as an overarching identity has been based on language and religion and, to some extent, on cultural style. Fulani ethnic identity has been based less on language or religion and more on lineage linkages.

This difference between Hausa and Fulani community criteria may reflect the fact that the Hausa are an assimilating ethnic community, while the Fulani – at least in Kano – have been exclusivist." – (John N. Paden, Berkeley: University of California Press, 1973, *Religion and Political Culture in Kano*, p. 378).

And whatever their origin is, there's ample evidence showing that their identity – Fulani identity – has also evolved through the years and even through the centuries because of cultural interactions and intermarriage with other groups.

The situation is similar to the transformation of the Tutsi in a period of more than 400 years during which they have intermingled, interacted and intermarried with the Hutu in the Great Lakes regions after they migrated to the area from the north and possibly from Ethiopia. As Frank A. Salamone, professor of anthropology and sociology at Iona College, New Rochelle, New York, states in a work edited by Professor Kevin Shillington, *Encyclopedia of African History, Volume I*:

"The search for the origin of the Fulani is not only futile, it betrays a position toward ethnic identity that strikes many anthropologists as profoundly wrong.

Ethnic groups are political action groups that exist, among other reasons, to benefit their members. Therefore, by definition, the social organization, as well as cultural content, will change over time. Moreover, ethnic groups such as the Fulani, are always coming into, and going out of, existence.

Rather than searching for the legendary eastern origins of the Fulani, a more productive approach might be to focus on the meaning of Fulani identity within concrete historical situations and analyze the factors that shaped Fulani ethnic identity and the manner in which people used it to attain particular goals....

Their adoption of Islam increased the Fulani's feelings of cultural and religious superiority to surrounding peoples. That adoption became a major ethnic boundary marker....

Fulani Sirre, or town Fulani, never lost touch with their relatives, however, often investing in large herds themselves. Cattle remain a significant symbolic symbolic repository of Fulani values....

Holy wars – jihads – after their success...followed the basic principle of Fulani ethnic dominance....

For the fully nomadic Fulani, the practice of transhumance – the seasonal movement in search of water – strongly influences settlement patterns. The basic settlement, consisting of a man and his dependents, is called a *wuru*. It is social but ephemeral, given that many such settlements have no women and serve simply as shelters for the nomads who tend the herds.

There are, in fact, a number of settlement patterns among the Fulani. Since the late twentieth century, there has been an increasing trend toward livestock production and sedentary settlement, but Fulani settlement types still range from traditional nomadism to variations on sedentarism.

As the modern nation-state restricts the range of nomadism, the Fulani have adapted ever increasingly complex ways to move herds among them. Over tha last few centuries, the majority of Fulani have become sedentary.

Those Fulani who remain nomadic or seminomadic have two major types of settlements: dry-season and wet-season camps. The dry season lasts from about November to March, the wet season from about March to the end of October.

Households are patrifocal and range in size one nuclear family to more than one hundred people.

The administrative structure, however, crosscuts patrilines and is territorial. Families tend to remain in wet-season camps while sending younger males – or, increasingly, hiring non-Fulani herders to accompany the cattle to dry-season camps." – (Frank A. Salamone, in Kevin Shillington, ed., *Encyclopedia of African History, Volume 1,* Fitzroy Dearborn Publishers, Inc., 2005, pp. 534 – 535).

That's what they're. That's how they live. That's their culture. Even the Fulani who have abandoned the nomadic lifestyle and those who live in towns have not forgotten their brethren in the rural areas and the way they live. They identify with them.

There may be some differences but they are all Fulani united by a common identity even though there are still some disputes as to what a Fulani really is in terms of cultural and ethnic identity because of the changes Fulanis have undergone through the centuries; an assessment that applies to other groups as well.

Wolof

The Wolof, also known as Jollof, are the third-largest ethnic group in The Gambia after the Mandinka and the Fulani. Yet their influence in the country rivals that of the Mandinka, the largest group.

Like the Mandinka and the Fula, the Wolof transcend national boundaries. But they're united by a common identity as an ethnic group whose members share many characteristics, especially cultural.

And while they are all essentially Wolof, they are also divided by history.

The Wolof in The Gambia have been shaped by a different colonial experience – Anglophone – in sharp contrast with that of their brethren in Senegal and other Francophone countries.

The transnational Wolof identity also assumes other dimensions when it becomes Pan-African in the sense that it fosters solidarity with members of other groups by embracing them when they use or accept some Wolof cultural elements.

There is, for example, a transcendence that has been achieved by a phenomenon called Wolofisation even in the multicultural context of individual countries, especially Gambia and Senegal, where one component of Wolof identity predominates.

This is the linguistic component which assumes other dimensions as well, as a cultural force and as a tool of integration, spreading Wolof culture and drawing into the Wolof community, or orbit, people who are not ethnic Wolofs but who become "Wolof" because they use the Wolof language as a practical necessity. As stated in a book edited by Professor Andrew Simpson, *Language and National Identity in Africa*:

"As the Wolof language spreads and new urban immigrants start to use it on an everyday basis and in their own households, a generational linguistic shift to Wolof commonly occurs. In such contexts, when language and ethnicity become conflated, more and more people identify themselves as Wolof.

Being Wolof in an urban context can, however, mean many things since, as argued in McLaughlin (2001), Wolof is often used as a convenient term for an urban identity.

A telling example comes from a Haalpulaar schoolteacher from the town of Fatick (in Senegal) who claimed, 'When I am at home I am a Haalpulaar, when I am in Dakar I am a Wolof,' (McLaughlin: 156), by which he meant that in Dakar he is as fully integrated an urbanite as anyone else.

Paradoxically, however, the negative attributes of urban life have also been projected onto the concept of Wolof as both an ethnic group and as a language." – (Andrew Simpson, *Language and National Identity in Africa*, New York: Oxford University Press, 2008, p. 94).

And as the Wolof language becomes increasingly dominant in The Gambia, members of some ethnic groups may feel that their cultures are now being threatened or swamped by Wolofisation. As the Wolof language consolidates itself in many areas of national life, the Wolof culture also becomes more widespread; and so does Wolof influence in general.

But many non-Wolofs who speak Wolof are no more Wolofised when they speak Wolof than they are anglicised when they speak English.

That's because the Islamic culture is the dominant culture in The Gambia, as much as it is in Senegal, and indigenous cultures are also strong in their own ethnic contexts; with Wolof being one of the strongest and most resilient through the centuries, a phenomenon partly attributed to the large number of indigenous Wolofs in the region and their deep-rooted history as descendants of one of the most prominent precolonial states in Africa. As Professor G. Wesley Johnson of the History Department at Stanford University – his analysis is relevant in the context of Gambia as well, along with Senegal, since the Wolof community transcends national boundaries – states in his book *The Emergence of Black Politics in Senegal: The Struggle for Power in the Four Communes, 1900-1920*:

"The most numerous and important inhabitants of Senegal are the Wolofs, a proud, handsome people who have been the traditional masters of the northern and central heartland plain.

Through war, trade, empire, and marriage, Wolof has become the lingua franca of Senegal, spoken by over one-third and understood by possibly two-thirds of all Senegalese.

The Wolofs were the first Senegalese to meet Europeans; and they quickly became French auxiliaries, serving as traders, soldiers, sailors, and interpreters. Consequently, they were the earliest African dwellers in the French settlements.

The recorded history of the Wolof peoples does not extend as far back as that of the Toucouleurs. Some observers believe that the Wolofs once lived in Tekrour; others hold that they originated in Mauritania and later moved south.

There is also evidence that the Wolofs may have descended from from the Toucouleurs or Sereres – and may possibly be a mixture of both these ancient peoples.

The modern Wolof historian Cheikh Anta Diop has speculated that the Wolofs originated on the Upper Nile, basing his hypothesis on certain similarities in language and culture.

Oral tradition simply states that the Djolof empire of the Wolof peoples was founded in the thirteenth or fourteenth century by Ndiadiane N'Diaye, who may possibly have been the son of a Toucouleur cleric.

N'Diaye's reputation for bravery and supernatural powers led to his selection as the first Bourba of Djolof – i.e. Emperor of the Wolofs. Gaining control of Djolof and of Walo, the Wolof state near the mouth of the Senegal, he apparently united these with the Wolof states of Cayor and Baol to form the Djolof empire.

Soon Tekrour and the southern Serere kingdoms of Sine and Saloum became subject to the Wolof state, which also controlled Fulbe lands to the east and Malinke villages to the southeast.

At the beginning of the fifteenth century, after the demise of the Mali empire, Djolof embraced all of modern Senegal's heartland, creating a precedent for the French to build on four centuries later.

Wolof culture and language slowly spread to the vanquished peoples, especially in the upper classes, and diverse peoples on the periphery of Wolof culture were wholly or partially assimilated.

This process has continued to the present, in part because the Djolof empire, though vanished, still lends its prestige to today's Wolofs." – (G. Wesley Johnson, *The Emergence of Black Politics in Senegal: The Struggle for Power in the Four Communes, 1900-1920*, Stanford University Press, 1972, p. 9).

Probably the most visible symbol of that heritage is the Wolof language itself which is virtually synonymous with Wolof culture in terms of prominence and influence.

Closely related to Serer and Fulbe, the Wolof language is also a major means of communication in commercial activities in many areas outside Senegambia, such as Mali, Guinea and Mauritania.

In fact, the Wolof are some of the most prominent and most successful traders throughout West Africa. Many of them also have international ties, operating businesses in many parts of the world including New York and other major cities in the metropolitan West.

The largest number of Wolofs live in Senegal but a significant number of them also live in The Gambia. In fact, in terms of percentage and raw numbers, The Gambia has the second-largest population of Wolofs in the entire West Africa.

In The Gambia, they're dominant in the Greater Banjul area where the Wolof language is also used as the lingua franca. Apart from the Banjul area, the Wolof are also dominant north of the Gambia River in the upper and lower Saloum districts and the northern parts of Niani,

Sami, Niumi and Jokadu.

But that's not their original homeland anymore than other other parts of The Gambia are the original homelands of the other ethnic groups.

There are different versions about their origin which differ somewhat; sometimes complementing, reinforcing or contradicting each other in some areas. According to an article by Edward E. Carayol, "The Wolof," published in one of Gambia's newspapers, *Today*:

"It is believed that the Wolof language belongs to the Atlantic branch of the Niger-Congo language family.

As with many tribes in The Gambia, the Wolof language and peoples are found in The Gambia, Senegal and part of Mauritania, albeit it is known for its prevalence in The Gambia and its neighbour Senegal.

Wolof history probably dates to about the 12th or 13th century. Wolof forefathers migrated west to the coast from Mali following the defeat of the Empire of Ghana in the 11th century.

Oral family histories indicate that at least some of the first settlers in the area were of Fulbe origin.

Much Wolof history has been preserved in oral praise songs which are recited by griots ('professional praise singers').

Portuguese traveller accounts from the 15th century indicate an organized Wolof presence in what are still their homelands.

Europeans established a fort on Gorée Island off the coast of modern-day Dakar, which served as one of the primary points of departure for slaving vessels bound for the Americas.

Since European contact, Wolof history has undergone numerous conquests and revolts as competing rulers challenged one another for kingship.

The climate of the Wolof area varies greatly from north to south. The north is nearly desert-like, while the southern region is a tropical rain forest. The crops grown in each area reflect the climate of that zone.

Staple crops are sorghum and millet. Tomatoes, peppers, peanuts, and beans are also grown.

Fish is very important, and rice is a staple of urban Wolof diets.

Until the late 19th century, Wolof rulers played a key part in the slave trade, directing slave raids and selling captured individuals from inland peoples to the Europeans on the coast.

Origin and Migration

The Wolof are found mainly in the Senegambia region, in the area of Walo, Jolof, Kayor (Cayor) and parts of Baol and Sine in the Senegal region.

In The Gambia, the Wolof are found in Saloum, north of Niani, and in Upper Niumi, Baddibu and Jokadu.

The Wolof language can be regarded as the lingua franca of northern Senegambia. This is because it was the language of commerce and communication in the trading centres, especially those frequented by the Moors, Serer, Tukulor, Mandinka, and the many peoples who interacted with them.

The ancestors of the Wolof are believed to have migrated from the Sahara Desert area. They were one of the earlier peoples who inhabited this, now hostile region before it became a desert.

As the once-fertile land gradually dried up, the people began to move in different directions in search of environments that were more conductive to human habitation and agriculture.

According to tradition, the ancestors of the Wolof, during this period of forced migration gradually moved into the area north of Senegal, that became known as Futa Toro and Mauritania.

Between AD 639 and 642, the Arabs conquered Egypt

first, and then the rest of North Africa. They gradually forced the Berbers who originally lived in the area to move south, thus causing further southward migration.

At about the same time, the Fula moved from the east into Futa Toro. The ancestors of the Wolof were, in turn, forced to move from Mauritania and Futa Toro into northern and eastern Senegal.

As they moved, they forced the few Serer and Mandinka who settled in the area earlier to move into Sine, Saloum, and the upper Gambia regions. The Wolof then settled in small villages under chiefs (or *lamans*), each independent of the other.

It is believed that the villages gradually developed into states and kingdoms. One such kingdom was Jolof, which was later conquered in the mid-thirteenth century by the generals of Sundiata Keita, the Mandinka emperor of Ancient Mali. By the 14th century, Jolof was no longer a vassal of Mali because it, too, had formed its own empire.

The Jolof Empire

The Wolof called their empire Jolof. It housed the kingdoms or states of Jolof which was served as an overlord controlling Walo, Kayor, and Baol on the coast, Sine and Saloum, Serer states in the south, and finally Dimar, which was an inland state east of Walo.

It was believed that this empire was formed either by voluntary association, meaning all the states willingly agreed to form a single political entity, or by conquest – an empire – and accepted Jolof as their overlord.

Since it is unlikely that people or state would willingly give up their independence, it is assumed that member states agreed to form an empire because they were threatened by other powerful neighbours and felt more secured in a bigger entity; or that the kingdom of Jolof was powerful enough to conquer surrounding states.

Even though these states were tribute-paying vassals,

they maintained a great deal of independence, especially in political affairs. They sometimes contributed contingents to the army of Jolof and paid such tributes as salt, fish, and grass for thatching roofs of huts, and cattle. The weak control exercised by Jolof over her vassals was confirmed by early Portuguese explorers and traders.

As more Europeans traded with such coastal states as Kayor, Walo, and Baol, they became powerful enough to challenge the authority of their overlord. It was their fight for political independence that led to the final disintegration of the empire in 1566.

Kayor set the example by rebelling and gaining her independence. All the other vassal states followed her example. After this, Jolof tried very hard to rebuild the empire but she failed because the former vassal states were determined to maintain their newly earned freedom.

None of the former vassal states was able to build an empire in Jolof's place, although Kayor was able to absorb Baol and set up dual ruler-ship.

Each Wolof state was constantly occupied by its own internal problems and, at the same time, sought to maintain its independence from its neighbours. But with the increased presence of the Europeans, they had a new problem to contend with, and this was to keep the Europeans out of their internal political affairs.

Legend of Njanjan Njie

Njanjan Njie was believed to be the first ruler of Walo and founder of the Jolof empire. According to tradition, he was the son of Abu Bakr Ibn Mohamed and Fatimata Sal. He was called Amadu Bubakar Ibn Mohamed.

A few years after the death of his father, his mother, Fatimata Sal, remarried her husband's former slave, and Amadu Bubakar threw himself into the strong currents of the river as a sign of his total rejection of the marriage. Many believed him to be dead, but he survived because he was a good swimmer. He lived an almost amphibious life, hiding by the banks of River Senegal.

Legend has it that he eventually emerged from hiding because he wanted to prevent bloodshed among a group of fishermen of Mengen who were quarrelling over the distribution of firewood. The villagers were astonished by his appearance and thought that he was a genii or spirit from the river.

He further surprised them when he shared the firewood fairly and thus prevented bloodshed. He then disappeared, much to their dismay. The villagers decided to capture him, so they pretended to have another quarrel. When he appeared again to mediate, they captured him.

He refused to communicate with them, but his silence was broken by a beautiful woman who talked to him; she was later given to him in marriage.

In the meantime, the elders of the village had sent a delegation to a seer and diviner in the neighbouring state of Sine, who was also the ruler. He was called Mansa Wali Jon. On hearing this story, the king of Sine exclaimed, 'Njanjan Njie,' which in his native Serer language meant 'this is extra-ordinary.'

The delegation from the fishing village, on hearing this, concluded that it was the name of the stranger.

From that time, Amadu Bubakar became known as Njanjan Njie.

Mansa Wali Jon assured the people that the stranger was not a genii but that every state in the area should accept him as their overlord. He was the first to pledge his allegiance to Njanjan Njie. All the other leaders of the surrounding states followed his example. It was for this reason that people believed that the empire was formed by voluntary association.

Njanjan Njie returned to Walo and became the first ruler of the state. After governing for about sixteen years, he decided to go into self-exile because of growing dissatisfaction over his reign.

He went to the state of Jolof. Here he impressed the local chief with his dignity and intelligence, and he was made ruler to that state. His brother, Barka Mbody Wade, by his mother's second marriage continued to rule in Walo." – (Edward E. Carayol, "Wolof," in *Today*, Kanifing, The Gambia, 15 October 2009).

The different versions of Wolof history agree on one thing: The Wolof have a long history, and a culture that has been well-established for centuries. Their culture is also an integral part of their daily social and economic activities.

Although Wolofs are mostly farmers, many of them are also traders and fishermen. However, fishing is not their primary occupation as is the case with the members of some ethnic groups in the country such as the Serer. And as lifestyles are influenced by cultures including ways of earning a living, the economic activities in which the people are engaged also influence cultures, with agriculture being the most influential economic activity among the Wolof. It has played a major rule in shaping their culture through the centuries.

And their culture – values, customs, traditions and beliefs – has played a major role in shaping the Wolof traditional society.

It's a highly complex society based on the caste system comprising three castes: the freeborn including rulers and noblemen, the low caste comprising people with various skills such as metalsmiths, weavers and leather workers as well as griots; and slaves at the bottom of the social hierarchy. Household slaves usually became part of the family.

The caste system has had so much influence on Wolof society, and for so long, that its impact is felt even today. But there is also some dispute as to what really constituted th caste system among the Wolof. As Professor James F. Searing of the History Department at the University of

Illinois, Chicago, who also provides a re-interpretation of the caste system among the Wolof, disputing conclusions by other scholars who who contend that nobles and slaves – among other groups – belonged to castes – states in his book *West African Slavery and Atlantic Commerce: The Senegal River Valley, 1700 – 1860*:

"The origins of the Wolof 'caste" system are unknown, lost in the mists of times predating the formation of the monarchy.

The subdivision of Wolof society into free persons, hereditary occupational groups, and slaves, resembles similar hierarchies elsewhere in the western Sudan.

Although sometimes described as a caste system, the occupational groups in question form only a small segment of Wolof society; neither nobles, warriors, marabouts, slaves, or peasants belong to 'caste' groups, and most social distinctions based on wealth, learning, power or occupation fall outside the so-called 'caste' phenomenon.

Artisanal groups and *griot* groups have been described as castes for two reasons. There is a widespread belief in their social inferiority, accompanied by prejudice and superstitions about members of these groups. In addition, there are strictly observed rules of endogamy between *geer* ('non-caste') and *neeno*('caste'), who do not intermarry. Within the various groups of artisans intermarriage does occur, but intermarriage between artisans and *griots* is very rare.

The prejudices and marriage taboos which form the core of the 'caste' principle may be based on ancient religious beliefs, which are no longer fully incomprehensible.

Blacksmiths (*tegg*) are the most respected and feared occupational group, because of their command of fire and iron, their use of incantations (Wolof, *jatt*) and beliefs that they can bring bad luck. Blacksmiths may have once had a religious role, preserved today in the memory of their role in circumcision ceremonies and as keepers of rave sites.

Leatherworkers, who form the second artisan group, may also have once wielded some religious or magical power, represented in recent times by their fabrication of protective charms (Wolof, *teere*).

But in any case these beliefs appear to be remnants from the past. The Wolof ideology of caste is attenuated, compared to the more elaborate system of beliefs that defines caste in the less islamized Mane world.

Interpretations of 'caste' which emphasize social taboos and magico-religious beliefs can neglect the way that the 'caste' principle distributes political power, honor, and economic privilege.

The social charter of 'caste' denies political power and honor to the *neeno*, but rewards them with an economic monopoly in their respective professions.

The 'caste' principle sustains the social division of labor because no *geer* can perform any of the trades reserved to the *neeno*. Honor and power are reserved to the *geer*, a social group that includes the peasantry as well as the aristocracy.

'Caste' places agricultural communities at the center of the social world, the source of power and honor.

Caste groups participate in the world of power and honor only as clients. At the same time the caste principle obscured the class divisions between the aristocracy and the peasantry." – (James F. Searing, *West African Slavery and Atlantic Commerce: The Senegal River Valley, 1700 – 1860*, Cambridge University Press, 2003, p. 39).

Professor Searing goes on to state:

"In the period of the 'monarchy the 'caste' groups became hereditary client groups, attached to particular families. Over time the monarchy reshaped these groups into dependents who were attached to the court. The social relations between nobles and clients, based on inequality and the gifts given by the lord to his clients, came to define the caste system.

The demand for iron weapons, spears, daggers; and arrows, employed many smiths, who also learned how to repair European trade guns and to fabricate shot. Some blacksmiths specialized in the production of jewelry in gold and silver for aristocratic women, becoming a distinct subgroup in the blacksmith occupational occupational group.

Leatherworkers specialized in the production of saddles and harnesses for the horses of the aristocracy and in the production of handbags and decorative goods for aristocratic women.

Both blacksmiths and leatherworkers were given titled leaders who resided in royal capitals to assure the organization of production, but also to serve as courtiers with ceremonial functions and leaders who could mobilize blacksmiths and leatherworkers in time of war.

Apart from the artisan groups, most of the specialized client groups of the old regime were specialists in verbal arts, in music, or were courtiers by profession.

The Wolof commonly divide casted persons in two broad groups, the artisans (*jef-lekk*) who live by their crafts, and the courtiers and bards (*sabb-lekk*) who live by entertaining and flattering their patrons with words and music.

The courtiers and bards can in turn be subdivided into subgroups, each with a specialized function based on the instruments they played, the specialized knowledge they preserved, and the role they played at court.

As a group the bards (*gewel)* and courtiers (*noole*) were considered of baser origins than the artisans and subject to more contempt ans ridicule. These prejudices are explained in myths attributing 'impure' origins to these groups, but also reflected their social role as praise singers, entertainers, flatters and courtiers, the 'dogs of court' (Wolof, *xaju mbooloo*).

In social relations, the inferiority of bards and courtiers is expressed in their constant solicitation of gifts from their social superiors, who are obliged to reward their praises and entertainment with payments." – (Ibid., pp. 39 – 40).

The existence of such social superiors was a product of social divisions which were themselves a product of social inequality in a hierarchal society.

But such social differences, which amounted to discrimination, did not prevent the members of different castes from working together. In fact, the castes were structured in such a way that they functioned as interlocking mechanisms for the smooth functioning of the Wolod society, as was the case with other societies in Senegambia and other parts of West Africa which also had caste systems.

As a system structured on the basis of preconceived notions about the members of society, the caste system was inherently unequal. But it also ensured cultural continuity under rulers who believed in the stratified nature of society which assigned – for life – social status to its members.

It was also a complex society which could not be simply reduced to three divisions or be explained only in terms of the tripartite nature of the caste system. As Professor Megan Vaughan in the Faculty of History at Cambridge University states in her book *Creating the Creole Island: Slavery in Eighteenth Century Mauritius*:

"Wolof society...exhibited a tripartite division between the freeborn, those who were members of specific 'castes,' and slaves....The Wolof caste system displayed a classic combination of discrimination, taboo, and ambiguity. Hence members of the blacksmith caste were regarded as both powerful and a source of danger.

Though technically caste members occupied a rung in

the social ladder beneath that of all free persons, in parctice the situation was more complex.

In some circumstances the lower echelons of the free population, consisting of poorer peasants, had fewer social privileges than caste members. Similarly, within the category of slave there was also a hierarchy, with war captives lying at the bottom. The upper echelons of the slave category, the royal slaves, were a privileged and potentially powerful group, just as the equivalent group was some Malagasy states.

There was also a strong warrior tradition in Senegambia, which gave rise in the eighteenth century to the Wolof autocratic and militaristic *ceddo* regimes – themselves in part a consequence of the effects of the slave trade.

Though conflict might be ethnicized in this region, often it is difficult, if not impossible, to disentangle this from religious conflict. Jihads and conflicts between Moslems and non-Moslems constituted one of the dynamics producing slaves to be sold to the French. In this context ethnic identities might follow from rather than be prior to religious identifications. In any case, the two were so closely connected that that term *Bambara*, for example, might designate a non-Muslim.

Add to the religious differences and religious hierarchies an age-grade system and a kinship system, and one can begin to think that the Wolof might have regarded the society of *ancien régime* France as simple and egalitarian in its structure." – (Megan Vaughan, *Creating the Creole Island: Slavery in Eighteenth Century Mauritius*, Durham, North Carolina, USA: Duke University Press, 2004, p. 115).

From what we have just learnt, it's easy to see that the Wolof traditional society was one of the most complex in West Africa if not on the entire continent, and with a highly sophisticated, well-structured, hierarchy.

In the rigid traditional structure, if you were member of the low caste, you lived and died a member of the low caste. You were trapped for life and even married within your caste. And as Gambian author, Dr. Tijan M. Sallah, states in his book, *Wolof*:

"Wolof society was organized into a hierarchy of castes, a rigid structure in which the social position of a person was inherited. A person's caste could not be changed, no matter what his or her merits.

The Wolof caste system allowed members of the lower castes to achieve as much economic progress as the freeborn. In fact, many low castes were wealthier than their social superiors.

Today, however, the caste system is giving way to a society based on merit and achievement.

The Wolof had three main castes: *jambur* or *gor* (freeborn), *nyenyo* (artisan castes), and *jam* (slaves)." – Tijan M. Sallah, *Wolof*, Rosen Publishing Group, 1996, p. 27).

Distinctions in the tripartite system of castes – the high caste of the freeborn, the low caste of artisans, and the lowest caste of slaves – has been eroded through the years by modernisation including adoption of new values and changes in traditional beliefs.

Education and wealth have now become more important as determinants of social status not only among the Wolof but also among other indigenous groups in The Gambia.

But even today, the Wolof traditional society is strong, especially among the people in the rural areas. Urban dwellers are just as strong in their support of some aspects of their traditional culture.

Some of the most important practices which also reinforce Wolof identity – even among urban residents – include circumcision and naming ceremonies. They're rites of passage. You can not become a true Wolof in terms of maturity and identity without going through them. The practice of circumcision is also inextricably linked with Islam, the dominant religion and bedrock of society.

Elders also play a very important role in guiding the young. They serve as role models for both boys and girls, with boys looking up to men, and girls up to women who exemplify the best in the Wolof traditional society.

The Wolof also have tremendous respect for elders. Even among younger people, those who are older than others are respected.

Another very important aspect of life among the Wolf in the traditional society and even in the modern context is hospitality. Traditional hospitality among the Wolof is known as *terranga* and is strictly observed. It's against their culture not to share a meal with a visitor. Rudeness is rebuked. And the system of the extended family is an integral part of life among the Wolof as is the case in most traditional societies across Africa. As Professor Patricia Tang at the Massachusetts Institute of Technology (MIT) states in her book *Masters of the Sabar: Wolof Griot Percussionists of Senegal*:

"In discussing 'family,' in the case of the Wolof, I mean the extended family – for among the Wolof, the important kinship unit is not the conjugal family but rather a much wider group of relatives.

A household (*ker*) typically includes the eldest male as *borom-ker* (head of the household) and his first wife and children; but any number of other relatives may live there as well – siblings, nephews and nieces, grandchildren, and even fictive kin (with no actual blood ties).

The frequency of divorce and children born out of wedlodk further increases the number of dependents in a given family.

Thus, the notion of family should not be rigidly defined, but rather has ever-shifting boundaries, allowing for exceptions to the strict rule of blood lines.

The importance of the extended family is reflected in the Wolof vocabulary. For example, the word *mbokk* meaning 'relative,' is derived from the root *bokk*, 'to share.' The term *maam* is used for the class of grandparents and other ancestors; so no distinction is made between a grandfather and a grandfather's siblings.

Likewise, for people of the same generation, the words *mag* (elder) and *rakk* (younger) would be used, depending on the person's age relative to the speaker; however, there is no distinction of whether this person is a brother, sister, or cousin.

Thus, in a sense, every person in an older generation is a grandparent; likewise, every peer is a brother or sister. This lack of linguistic distinction promotes the inclusion of all relatives as 'family.'

In tracing kinship, the Wolof use a double descent or bilineal kinship structure. Although in former times, matrilineage was traditionally more important, the rapid spread of Islam in the late nineteenth century gave greater import to patrilineage.

Thus, today, although families tend to be patrifocal and children are given the last names of their fathers, both lineages are considered important. – (Patricia Tang, *Masters of the Sabar: Wolof Griot Percussionists of Senegal*, Philadelphia, Pennsylvania, USA: Temple University Press, 2007, pp. 57 – 58).

Central to existence of the extended family is the family unit or the nuclear family comprising the father, mother and children. It's forms the basic foundation of the extended family and of the traditional society from which everything else radiates.

There would be no extended family without strong family units upheld by traditional values of strong family ties, compassion and hospitality.

And critical to the proper functioning of the family unit

is the role of the father and of the mother or – in the absence of either one – of the oldest member in the household; for example, the oldest son or daughter.

Wolof society is patrilineal. It also has matrilineal elements in terms of inheritance among others. It's also patrifocal: the father is the centre of authority. He's also the final arbiter in all family disputes in his household over which he has full jurisdiction.

The mother is equally important but mainly in terms of managing the household – cooking, taking care of the children, going to the market and so on.

The mother is also important in another fundamental respect which has nothing to do with daily activities. It has to do with genes:

"The Wolof believe that a person inherits from the mother's side blood (*deret*), flesh (*soox*), character (*jiko*), and intelligence (*xel*) (Abdoulaye-Bara Diop, 1981, 19).

Certain serious illnesses such as leprosy are considered hereditary through the mother's side; likewise, witchcraft (*ndemm*), the ability to kill and eat the souls of other human beings, is also inherited from the mother.

From the father, one receives bones (*yax*), nerves (*siddit*), and courage (*fit*); supernatural vision (*nooxoor*) can also be inherited from the father, but no other witchcraft powers may be inherited from him (Diop 1981, 20).

A child is thought to inherit more from his mother than from his father, as blood, flesh, character, and intelligence are arguably more important than bones, nerves, and courage.

The ubiquitous explanation that Wolof *gewel* (griot) provide in reference to how they can play sabar, 'it's in my blood,' reflects a matrilineal inheritance. Thus, although a young *gewel* most likely learns to play sabar from his father or other male relatives in his family, he is also able to inherit drumming from his mother's side." – (Ibid., p.

58).

It's true that both men and women play important roles in Wolof culture. But it's also equally true that it's a male-dominated society, best exemplified by the prerogative men exercise to marry more than one wife, a practice that's resented by a significant number of women especially modern ones. Even some women in the traditional society resent that.

But, as in other tribes, polygyny – commonly known as polygamy – is common, a traditional practice in perfect accord with the dominant religion among the Wolof and most Gambians, Islam, which allows men to have more than one wife.

Traditionally, parents have played a major role in the selection of spouses for their children among the Wolof. The mother plays this role more than the father does in most cases. but there is resistance to this practice among modernised Wolofs, the educated and urban dwellers, who prefer to choose their own spouses.

It has also been a traditional practice to look for a spouse within one's social class – which is rooted in the caste system – but many young people cross these boundaries.

Still, as in most societies, people of higher social status usually don't marry those in the lower classes, although it does happen. But it's mostly men who do that. It's rare to find a woman of higher social status who has married a man of lower status.

However, modernisation continues to blur these social distinctions. But modernisation has also come at a price. It has had a negative impact on the traditional society through the years, leading to erosion of traditional values including morality, especially among the young, with urban dwellers being some of the biggest "offenders."

But even with all these changes, it's critical to remember that the Wolof have remained intact through the centuries as an ethnic entity, with its own identity, a socio-cultural continuity attributed to their strong culture.

The most outstanding features of Wolof society which unite the people include resilience of their cultural identity through the centuries; a strong sense of ethnic identity and solidarity; a common language; a common religion, Islam; traditional patterns of kinship; traditional institutions of authority which act as spiritual and socio-political anchors; and traditional beliefs across the spectrum, including religious, a major cultural component even Islam has not been able to neutralise let alone eradicate. It remains an integral part of the traditional way of life even among the elite.

Adherence to both is not seen as a contradiction between the two. In fact, many people follow both, simultaneously, remaining true to their indigenous beliefs while at the same time accepting the validity and legitimacy of an imported religion just as Christians do.

In fact, both Islam and Christianity are alien to Africa in spite of attempts by some Africans to indiginise the two religious faiths in terms of origin. What can be indiginised is adaptability of the two religions, but not their origin. The origin of both is the Middle East, not Africa.

But Islam has had such an impact on the Wolof – and on other ethnic groups as well – that a Christian among them especially in a traditional village would be an anomaly and a kind of social outcast.

Islam not only regulates life; it has become the national culture and the dominant culture of the Wolof. The cultures of other ethnic groups – except of the descendants of freed slaves known as the Aku or Creole – have also been Islamised in many ways.

And none of the indigenous cultures is pure even without the influence of Islam. They all have been influenced by other cultures, have borrowed elements from other cultures, and share many traits and characteristics with the other indigenous cultures. They're not pure even as ethnic entities. The Wolof, for example, have Mandingo, Serer and Fula elements incorporated into their ethnic group through the centuries and are therefore not pure Wolof.

Therefore all these groups and cultures are also partly a product of other groups and cultures.

But in spite of all that, all these groups and cultures have distinctive characteristics. That's why there is, for example, Wolofisation of other ethnic groups not only in terms of language but also in terms of culture. Many non-Wolofs in the highly urbanised Greater Banjul area have been Wolofised.

The Wolof have demonstrated a capacity to influence other people, incorporate into their culture elements from outside, adapt to changes, and at the same time retain their distinctive cultural identity as Wolof.

Jola

The Jola are the fourth-largest ethnic group in The Gambia after the Mandinka, the Fula, and the Wolof. They also live in the Casamance Province in neighbouring Senegal and in the northern part of Guinea-Bissau where they're known as Diola.

In The Gambia, they live mostly in the Foni areas south of Bintang Bolon in the Western Division in the southwestern part of the country.

They're among the most traditionally conservative people not only in The Gambia but in the entire West Africa. Village life is very important in their culture. They form settlements based on the extended family.

They also have strong sub-group identities which collectively constitute their ethnic identity that's expressed in many ways including traditional dances.

Their tribal structure is not hierarchal. Traditionally, they don't have strong central authority as in many traditional societies across Africa. Theirs is a highly decentralised society composed of autonomous units, each occupying its own area.

The situation is analogous to what the British colonial rulers found among the Igbo in Eastern Nigeria where there were no chiefs in a society that was highly egalitarian and centred on the clan system. As British historian Margery Perham stated when she wrote about the Nigerian civil war in *Africa Contemporary Record: Annual Survey and Documents 1968 – 1969*:

"As the British presence was drawn irresistibly further inland, it met the more isolated groups, and above all the numerous Ibo people.

The physical conditions of Africa have made possible the virtual isolation from fully effective contacts with other peoples of large populations with resulting sharp contrasts in civilization.

The wet forests east of the Niger hindered the entry of other peoples, especially the warlike slave-raiding, horse and cattle people of the north (Hausa-Fulani), but the dividing forests also prevented the Ibo developing any political organisation above above the limited family or clan grouping.

To the British officials they seemed at once the most backward and the most intractable group of any size they had met in West Africa, and all attempts failed to find or create any form of chieftainship through which the administration could effectively administer these millions.

The Niger Coast Protectorate was proclaimed in 1891. Yet, when I studied the Ibo administration forty years later, the British officials were still groping for some structure through which to advance a group regarded as the most difficult and backward in Nigeria....Add to this that their lack of chiefs and cities (unlike the Yoruba and the Hausa-Fulani) gave them an equalitarian unity." – (Margery Perham, "Nigeria's Civil War," in Colin Legum and John Drysdale, *Africa Contemporary Record: Annual Survey and Dcouments 1968 – 1969*, London: Africa Research Limited, 1969, p. 3).

Not only do the Jolas have a social organisation similar to that of the Igbos; they also don't have a caste system. That's in sharp contrast with other ethnic groups such as the Mandinka and the Wolof who, traditionally, have had highly elaborate social structures and caste systems.

Their administration is, instead, conducted at the village level, with no higher authority than that. It is, in fact, one of the best examples of democracy in the African traditional context before the coming of Europeans.

Ironically, the Jola have – in spite of their traditional democratic society – produced one of the most undemocratic leaders in Africa in modern times, Yahya Jammeh, whose authoritarian instincts have helped him perpetuate himself in office since 1994 when he overthrew a democratically leader, President Dawda Jawara, who had ruled The Gambia for 30 years.

Jammeh is the most prominent Jola in the nation's history. And he has won rigged elections since the 1990s. At this writing, in 2010, he showed no signs of relinquishing power.

The cultural life of the Jola is inextricably intertwined with their economic activities which not only sustain individuals but the society as a whole.

Apart from being known as very good fishermen, the Jola are also farmers. They grow a lot of rice among other crops. In fact, in Jola traditional society, rice has been used as a measure of wealth and success. Those who grow more rice than others are considered to be wealthier.

The Jola are also known for collecting honey and tapping palm wine.

All these economic activities reinforce their identity, and partly determine their distinctive lifestyle as an ethnic group which also cherishes solidarity.

The freedom the Jola have enjoyed traditionally is also

one of the most distinctive features of their society.

Even the village head does not have power over his people besides acting as nominal head and as an arbitrator in disputes.

The degree of freedom and independence traditionally enjoyed by the Jola is clearly evident even in times of war.

Historically, villages mobilised forces during war. But as soon as the war ended, each village went back to minding its own business. The heads of different villages never formed a permanent alliance even though they were led by one warrior during war.

The Jola have a long history, being some of the first inhabitants in the area that's now known as The Gambia. But their history is shrouded in the mists of the past because they don't have griots as other tribes do.

And their existence in isolated areas – forested and swampy – severely limited their interaction with other people. They couldn't reach out and outsiders couldn't get in. But the people were obviously satisfied living that way in isolation. Otherwise they could have ventured out in large numbers to mingle and interact with the members of other tribes.

This kind of living arrangement also provided them with security. It also led to cultural isolation and made it very difficult for the Jola to have cultural exchanges with the members of other ethnic groups.

They were also among the last people in the region to be affected by European influence because of their isolation in the forests and swampy areas.

The biggest impact on their lives came when they were attacked by Islamic forces during the Jihad from 1850 to 1890.

The Jola resisted the attacks and conversion to Islam. They stuck to their traditional religious – animist – beliefs and were the most difficult people to convert to Islam. Although they later did, under sustained pressure by the Jihadists, many Jolas even today practise their traditional beliefs in spite of the fact that they're Muslim.

This was also the beginning of the end of their isolation – at least part of it – and many of them started to engage in other economic activities they had never been engaged in before: tapping palm wine, growing groundnuts, yams and other food crops, and owing livestock. These changes started taking place in the 1880s.

But their culture remained essentially the same in spite of the foreign influence that was starting to affect them, although very slowly.

One of the major changes in their traditional lifestyle was the introduction of chiefs under the system of indirect rule which was first practised by the British colonial rulers in Northern Nigeria.

The chiefs who were imposed on them were Mandinka. Their primary function was to collect taxes and act as intermediaries between the Jola and the colonial administrators. The Jola also had a native administrative body but subject to higher authority that was not Jola; it was British assisted by Mandinka chiefs.

But the British had a hard time administering the Jola. They were fiercely independent, and their society was not organised in a way that would have facilitated colonial administration.

It was not until the early 1900s that they grudgingly accepted British rule and began to have their own chiefs appointed by the colonial rulers to replace Mandinka chiefs.

It's another strange irony that the people who were most resistant to modernisation also produced the country's president, Yahya Jammeh, who is leading The Gambia by using modern – not traditional – institutions of authority.

But their adherence to traditional forms of leadership, even if not sophisticated with highly developed institutions as in other ethnic groups, and the egalitarian nature of their society, have all been well-documented with empirical evidence; a phenomenon that distinguishes the Jola from their neighbours in a remarkable way even though there are some disputes on this egalitarianism because the Jola also participated in slavery, thus instituting a hierarchy.

Senegalese scholar Mamadou Diouf has argued along those lines; an argument that may have been advanced by others as well.

Yet, even their participation in slavery did not undermine the egalitarian nature of their society because domestic slaves in their midst were adopted and became members of the family that adopted them. As Professor Linda Jane Beck of the Political Science Department at the University of Maine stated when she wrote about egalitarianism and decentralised political authority in precolonial Jola society in her book *Brokering Democracy in Africa: The Rise of Clientelist Democracy in Senegal*:

"The Jola...are widely viewed as distinctive in their absence of social stratification....Although Catherine Boone (2003: 1054) accurately states that 'there is more to [Jola] social organization than 'lack of hierarchy," in a comparison with other...ethnic groups, this is by far the most distinctive and generalizable attribute....

Although the Jola are characterized by their 'incredible diversity, to such a point that one cannot speak of the Jola except in terms of a geographic reference' (Darbon 1988: 31), Jola societies have been uniformly marked by an absence of hierarchical categories of social status. Unlike the Wolof and Tukulor, the Jola have never had a caste system based on ascribed occupations and endogamy, nor a class of slaves (Mark 1985; Pélissier 1966; Roche 1971; Thomas 1958). Pélissier (1966: 682) noted:

> All Jolas are socially equal and none is privileged nor has the obligation to fulfill particular functions that are conferred on him due to a definitive vocation that places him in the service of the collective.
> Jola society is ignorant of castes as it is ignorant of slavery;

nowhere does one find warriors, griots, leatherworkers, metalworkers, attached to their function by their birth, inheritor of techniques immutably transmitted from father to son, constrained from marrying except a girl from the same caste.

Without denying that these social structures are distinctive, Mamadou Diouf is critical of an idealization of Jola egalitarian societies in contrast to the inherently hierarchical northern societies, a romanticism and exoticism evident in colonial texts and ethnographies of the region....

Diouf (2001: 179 – 181) sets out to refute this ethnographic stereotype by drawing upon Peter Mark's (1985) ethnographic history of Lower Casamance to demonstrate the involvement of the Jola in slave raiding and the Atlantic slave trade (see also Baum 1999; Linares 1987).

Their involvement in slave raiding challenges the romanticized 'idyllic vision' of Jola societies, but without undermining the assertion of their distinctive egalitarianism given the common practice among the Jola of 'forced adoption." – (Linda Jane Beck, *Brokering Democracy in Africa: The Rise of Clientelist Democracy in Senegal*, Palgrave Macmillan, 2008, pp.162 – 163).

Adoption of slaves is one of the strongest arguments against the assertion that the Jola were not egalitarian. And as Professor Beck goes on to state:

"Mark (1987: 27) notes that a captive among the Jola 'was quickly regarded as a member of the adopting lineage and could, if a male, inherit his own rice fields from his adoptive family.'

In contrast to northern societies where certain families are still identified with a slave caste, forced adoption of slaves in Lower Casamance 'usually entailed few enduring social handicaps,' evidenced by the absence of any contemporary references among the Jola to individuals, their families, or their ancestors as slaves.

In contrast, Wolof and Tukulor informants privately identified the families of slave caste in a community, and on numerous occasions I observed the technically free 'slaves' of a *toorodo* family performing menial tasks such as sweeping the courtyard or disposing of garbage. When asked who these individuals were, they replied in a matter-of-fact manner that 'they are our family's slaves.'" – (Ibid., pp. 163 – 164).

There is also evidence showing that the absence of griots among the Jola demonstrated the existence of a non-hierarchical society whose socio-political authority was not highly decentralised:

"There are no lineage genealogies of noble families whose praises are sung by a caste of griots that could provide a Jola kinship group with a historical claim to power. Thus, unlike the Wolof and Tukulor dynasties, there has never been a ruling class of noble families among the Jola.

Furthermore, there was no precolonial Jola state, but 'rather a plurality of zones of politico-religious influence' (Thomas 1968: 1). Political power was highly dispersed, with the gerontocracy of each Jola village selecting a chief without obligations to a broader regional authority.

Even at the village level, the power of a Jola chief was constrained by the authority by the head of each concession or household in the village. Consequently, the Jola have historically had a very restricted notion of both authority and community.

Intermittently, Jola villages did contract alliances. But these agreements were ephemeral, often the result of external threats or the particular qualities of an individual chief, rather than groundwork for a Jola state. Once the enemy was pushed back or the leader disappeared, each group reclaimed its autonomy.

Even in the few instances where several villages united under a 'king,' or on occasion a 'queen,' their authority was typically circumscribed both geographically and politically.

A Jola king, or more accurately 'priest,' was a local religious figure who was appointed to serve as the guardian of the *boekin* (sacred object) of a particular village or group of villages. Unlike the prominent marabout leaders..., the political influence of a Jola king-priest was typically weak and their economic power mediocre at best (Pélissier 1966: 677 – 680).

Forced to bow to numerous and rigorous customs, the life of a Jola king was 'hardly enviable...a difficult responsibility that one sought to avoid' (Roche 1985: 35)."
– (Ibid., p. 164).

Their culture of resistance played a major role not only in delaying penetration of foreign influence into their territory; it also reinforced their identity in a distinctive way contrasted with other groups.

And although the majority of the Jola are now Muslim, there is also a small minority of Catholics among them. The adoption of these foreign religious faiths has also partly shaped their identity and culture in the modern context. But they still have a reputation of being resistant to external influence.

Also, because of their highly conservative nature and strict adherence to traditional beliefs, they may even have the highest percentage of animists among all the groups in The Gambia.

In fact, their isolation even led to marginalisation. They played only a peripheral role, if any, in the political arena before and after independence; a point underscored in a work by Arnold Hughes and David Perfect, *Historical Dictionary of The Gambia*:

"At independence, the Jola remained a socially excluded community, with many urban working as unskilled laborers. They were also eclipsed by other ethnic communities politically until the emergence of the Jola, Yahya Jammeh, as junta leader in the coup of 1994. Jola are now thought to be strongly represented in the Gambia National Army." – Arnold Hughes and David Perfect, *Historical Dictionary of The Gambia*, The Scarecrow Press, Inc., Fourth Edition, 2008, p. 121).

They're also strongly represented in the government. They're even over-represented in many areas because of tribalism practised by President Jammeh and his Jola brethren.

But for the vast majority of the Jola, life has remained basically the same. They still live in the rural areas. And they still live the traditional way of life which has changed little in centuries.

Even what they make, grow and produce, for example rice which is central to their existence, has a religious dimension and spiritual significance in their lives. It's all tied to the land, the abode and resting place of their ancestors. It's also inextricably linked with the spiritual world. Anything produced in abundance is seen as a blessing of their ancestors.

When something bad happens, they invoke the power of their ancestors, a belief and practice common in traditional religious beliefs across the continent.

In the case of the Jola, some of their traditional beliefs are in accord with Islam, while animists among them adhere to these beliefs even without Islam. Traditional beliefs predate Islam and Christianity. Yet there is no conflict. In fact, Christianity is more widespread among the Jola that it is among other ethnic groups in The Gambia. And it exists side by side with traditional religious beliefs just like Islam does:

"Even those Jola who are Muslim tend to be heavily influenced by traditional animist beliefs and practices. Jola wrestlers, for example, famous for their strength and skill, would not consider entering a tournament without first visiting a sacred crocodile pool and seeking *jujus* and magical potions from a *marabout*." – Emma Gregg and Richard Trillo, *The Rough Guide to The Gambia*, Rough Guides, 2003, p. 246).

The Jola also have other distinctive characteristics which reinforce their cultural identity:

"Unlike the Wolof social hierarchy, Jola society is segmented and flexible, with no lower castes....
Traditional dress for Jola men is shirts or waistcoats with huge baggy trousers, while women wear long strings of beads crossed from each shoulder to the opposite hip.
Unusually (sic) for a West African tribe, the Jola do not have a strong oral tradition; they have plenty of traditional music, but no *griots* to act as praise-singers and historians....
Traditionally, the Jola are farmers, hunters, fishermen and palm wine tappers. Most palm wine tappers are Manjago, a subsection of the Jola tribe originally from Guinea-Bissau, who are usually animist or Christian rather than Muslim....Because their practices run so contrary to Muslim tradition, their compounds are often semi-isolated on the fringes of villages....
The (Jola) tribe is currently in meteoric ascent, in profile, confidence and influence, since President Jammeh is a Jola and he has favoured many of his kin with prestigious positions in public life." – (Ibid., pp. 246 – 247).

Although the Jola are well-known for their strong traditional religious beliefs, they are not unique in that respect. Gambia's general population lives in both worlds in terms of worship. There is the traditional; and there is the world of imported religions: Islam and Christianity. And they live side by side without conflict:

"The main religion in The Gambia is Islam and around 90% of the population are Muslim. The remaining 10% are Christian and there's also a small minority of people who still believe in traditional forms of religion such as animism.

As with most things Gambian, there is a distinct lack of inter-religious animosity within the country, and everyone is free to worship how and who they want, without prejudice. We have personally found that Christians and Muslims mix very well and there is nothing but a healthy curiosity about each other's methods of worship and beliefs.

Some traditional beliefs are still widely held throughout the population. These include the protective powers of *jujus* which are worn by nearly everyone. There are also strong beliefs in the continuing existence of dragons, witches, etc.

This may sound medieval to Westerners but we should remember that we were still burning witches at the stake a few hundred years ago.

On the African continent these beliefs are still very potent and are an integral and important part of the way of life and The Gambia is no exception.

Although there is a strong Islamic and Christian influence in The Gambia today, many practices originating from past animist beliefs remain. Indeed, much behaviour is still governed by superstitious beliefs that endow natural objects and phenomena, idols, fetishes and individuals with supernatural forces or the power to protect or to use such forces. Some might say that this is not so far removed from Westerners' point of view when one considers the number of people who consult a daily horoscope and avidly watch horror movies.

You will see that many Gambians, from tiny babies to old citizens, wear amulets, commonly called *jujus*, on their body around the waist, neck, arms or legs. The *jujus* are often leather packets, or cowrie shells, which contain writings from the Koran as a spell, or charm, which is said to protect the wearer.

The *juju* will have been provided either at birth, naming or initiation ceremonies by the local *griot*, or animist priest. Alternatively, the spell or charm may have been prescribed by a *marabout*.

Gambians consult *marabouts* for a variety of reasons but the following are the most common: to protect against evil spirits; to improve one's status; or to remedy a situation. Such is the belief in these men that we were almost crushed in a human riot when a particularly famous *marabout* boarded the Banjul to Barra ferry, and all the passengers wanted to touch him.

In addition to the special powers of *jujus*, Gambians also have quite rigid beliefs in taboos and superstitions, although there is much variation in these beliefs from tribe to tribe, and from village to village." – (Craig Emms, linda Barnett, and Richard Human, *The Gambia*, Bradt Travel Guides; 2nd Edition, 2006, pp. 22 – 23).

It's a remarkable feat that a large number of Jolas have retained their indigenous beliefs and strictly follow them, while they – at the same time – profess and practise with religious zeal other faiths: Islam or Christianity.

One of the most distinctive features of their traditional religion is the preservation of some forests and other areas – including ponds, for example, crocodile pods – which they consider to be sacred and necessary in order to be able to communicate with spirits for guidance and protection.

But the concept of one supreme being was not alien to the Jola when Islam and Christianity were introduced to them. It was an integral part of their traditional religion.

One subgroup of the Jola, known as Jola Kasa, is highly observant of the old traditional ways and has rejected Christianity and Islam. Among all the Jola subgroups, it's the most conservative and most traditional, one of the very few who have remained true to their African identity totally rejecting foreign influence.

One of the old traditional practices, besides African religion, is polygamy. Many Jola men have more than one wife. It's common to find those who have four wives. Some men have even more than that.

The Jola also marry cousins, a practice not common in all traditional societies across Africa.

Jola men are also allowed to marry the wives of their brothers who have died, a practice that may be more widespread than is generally known in different parts of the continent.

The Jola also have a very strong system of communal interdependence. Village members help each other probably more than members of other tribes do. The extended family is also well-preserved and very strong among the Jola.

The close-knit nature of their traditional society makes it difficult even today for foreign influence to spread among the Jola.

And as in most traditional societies across Africa, both men and women work hard on the farm. Gender roles are clearly defined.

Land is extremely important in the lives of the Jola not only as a source of sustenance but also as a spiritual asset connecting the living and their departed ancestors.

The Jola may not have achieved much in terms of Western civilisation. And they may not be among the most modernised Africans. But they have been able to retain their essence as an indigenous people and as Africans probably more than many other people not only in The Gambia but on the entire continent.

Questions have been raised about their identity as an ethnic group. Other groups have, of course, been subjected to the same kind of "microscopic" scrutiny only in varying degrees. But they do exist as a group and as an ethnic entity: the Jola.

They speak the same language. They share cultural traits including values, customs and traditions, and traditional religious beliefs. And they have the same history. All those attributes collectively constitute criteria which determine their identity as an ethnic group.

Yet, questions persist, not only about the Jola but other groups as well, in different contexts, because the concept of ethnicity is problematic in spite of its legitimacy as an analytical tool in the study of different groups. As Professor Peter Mark of Wesleyan University states in his book *"Portuguese" Style and Luso-African Identity: Precolonial Senegambia, Sixteenth – Nineteenth Centuries*:

"In some instance, migrations and the attendant assimilation of earlier inhabitants by more recent arrivals have altered the local cultural map. This is the case with the formerly 'Bagnun' populations of the Gambia-Soungrougrou region and of the Fogny, north of the Casamance River.

In other instances, the labels associated with particular groups have changed, a process that also reflects the gradual coalescing, on the level of group identification, of several local populations...into a geographically more extensive group. This is the situation with the Floups of Fogny, who in the course of the nineteenth century came to be identified as 'Yolas' or 'Diolas' (English: Jolas).

Today the Jolas are described as an ethnic group. Members of this group now widely assert Jola identity.

The term Diola is a nineteenth-century concept that is closely tied to the French colonial presence – administrators, missionaries, and anthropologists – (in

Senegal); before about 1900 the ancestors of the Diolas would not have considered themselves as such. The ancestors of the present-day Diola were formerly often called the Floups. No one calls them that today, least of all themselves. – (Peter Mark, *"Portuguese" Style and Luso-African Identity: Precolonial Senegambia, Sixteenth – Nineteenth Centuries*, Bloomington, Indiana, USA: Indiana University Press, 2002, pp. 5 – 6. See also Ferdinand de Jong, "The Making of Jola Identity: Jola Inventing Their Past and Future," in *Proceedings CERES/CNWS*, Utrecht, Netherlands: CERES, 1995).

Professor Mark goes on to state:

"There are as many as ten subgroups of Diolas, distinguished mostly on the basis of language dialects. The national dialect of the Diola language is Diola Fogny; the people who live in Fogny, north of the Casamance River and south of The Gambia, are also called Diola-Fogny. Their neighbors to the west, in Buluf, are, not surprisingly, the Diola-Buluf....

So, in brief, many or most Diolas have Floup ancestry. One would not distinguish between Floups and Diolas. A few mid-nineteenth-century sources do that, but those writers existed at an historical moment when the appellation 'Floup' was just being replaced by the term 'Diola.' By the turn of the twentieth century, the term 'Diola' had taken on a broader meaning that included all the speakers of Diola dialects, and approximated what we would perhaps call an ethnic group.

Given the recent creation of Jola ethnicity, how does one refer to those seventeenth-century ancestors who themselves had no sense of being Jola?

It is clearly advisable to avoid the proleptic use of later ethnic labels. However, alternative appellations, such as 'the ancestors of the Jola,' are awkward, and they oversimplify the complex interactions that led to the creation of the present cultural and linguistic group.

Nevertheless, the admittedly awkward circumlocution 'ancestors of' is preferable because it is less ahistorical than the anachronistic use of contemporary ethnic labels." – (Ibid., p. 6).

The changes which take place through centuries and even in shorter periods make it difficult to specifically identify groups which have undergone those changes, especially when they absorb members of other groups or when they merge with other groups to form bigger groups or entities.

Question then arise: Exactly whom are we dealing with? How do the people identify themselves? Are they really just one ethnic group or tribe or is it several of them who have not even yet lost their original identities? And if they have assumed a new identity, what is it?

Professor Mark asks a related question and goes on to state:

"The history of cultural interaction and evolution of cultural identity evokes a related question:

Do contemporary identity concepts have meaning when applied retroactively across four centuries of time?

The concept 'ethnic group' is a relatively recent creation. The development and application of ethnic labels was often, as is now widely recognized by historians and anthropologists, a product of the colonial period. In this limited sense of the term, many contemporary Senegambian ethnic groups did not exist before the nineteenth century.

If, on the other hand, one defines 'ethnic group' as a population whose members speak a common language or closely related dialects, exhibit a common social organization, share religious rituals – except in the case of differential conversion to Islam and Christianity – and perceive themselves as constituting a common identity, then one could reasonably argue that such groups did exist long before the colonial period. In this sense, socio-cultural groupings analogous to contemporary 'ethnic groups' have a demonstrable historical depth in Senegambia." – (Ibid., pp. 6 – 7).

Such groups, or tribes or ethnic groups, did exist not only in Senegambia but in most parts of Africa before the coming of Europeans.

The Jola were one such group regardless of what they called themselves back then and even if they did not call themselves Jola.

But they did exist before the coming of Europeans as a collective entity with a common language, customs and and traditions and other attributes which identified them as one people and with the same history.

The Jola not only meet the criteria which determine ethnic identity, past and present; they're probably the oldest group, not just one of the oldest, in The Gambia.

Serahule

The Serahule are the fifth-largest ethnic group in The Gambia. Also known as Serahuli, Sarahuli, Sarakole, Serakule or Soninke, they are some of the most well-known people in West Africa because of their rich history and role as traders.

Highly organised traders among them became famous in West Africa and consituted a Serahule subgroup known as Wangara.

The term "Wangara" is used even today in different parts of West Africa – such as Ghana and Burkina Faso – to identify Serahules who live in urban areas where they're involved in trade and other activities. It's virtually synonymous with "Serahule."

The Serahule are one of the oldest ethnic groups in

West Africa. They were also among the first people in West Africa to convert to Islam.

They also occupy an important place in the history of West Africa as the founders of the old Ghana Empire.

They're found in many parts of West Africa and beyond but mainly in Mali, The Gambia, Senegal, Burkina Faso, Guinea-Bissau, Mauritania, Ivory Coast, Ghana, Sierra Leone, Cameroon and even in Nigeria.

Outside West Africa, they're also found in the Central African Republic, Gabon, Congo Republic which is also known as Congo-Brazzaville; in the Democratic Republic of Congo, formerly known as Zaire, and elsewhere.

They're small minorities in all those countries except Mali.

Mali has the largest number of Serahules in West Africa and on the entire continent. They're known as Soninke in Mali and in other countries.

Soninke traders are known as *dyula* or *jula* in West Africa and other parts. They're some of the most successful traders on the African continent, and the most successful in The Gambia where they're called Serahule. As stated in a work edited by Phillipe Aghion, professor of economics at Harvard Univesity, and Steven N. Durlauf, professor economics at the University of Wisconsin-Madison, *Handbook of Economic Growth, Volume 1A*:

"Ethnic differentials are common....The ethnic dimension of rich trading elites is well-known: the Lebanese in West Africa, the Indians in East Africa, and the overseas Chinese in Southeast Asia.

Virtually every country has its own ethnographic group noted for their success. For example, in the Gambia a tiny indigenous ethnic group called the Serahule is reported to dominate business out of all proportion to their numbers – they are often called 'Gambian Jews.'

In Zaire (now Democratic Republic of Congo), Kasaians have been dominant in managerial and technical jobs since the days of colonial rule – they are often called 'the Jews of Zaire' (*The New York Times*, 9/18/1996)." – (Phillipe Aghion and Steven N. Durlauf, eds., *Handbook of Economic Growth, Volume 1A*, North Holland, First Edition, 2006, p. 1035).

Other groups such as the Mandinka and the Wolof are also actively involved in business. But considering their size in Gambia's total population, the Serahule stand out among all the groups in the country because they have achieved success out of all proportion to their numbers.

The Serahule settled in large numbers in The Gambia from the 1850s, fleeing from wars in the region. Many of them also went to The Gambia to look for jobs and stayed.

They have their own identity as a distinct ethnic group but are also a mixture of the Mandinka, the Fula, and the Berbers.

In The Gambia, they're found mostly in the extreme Upper River region – which is the eastern part of the country – where they constitute the largest ethnic group. The highest concentration of the Serahule population is in the town of Basse located in the easternmost part of The Gambia.

The area where they live was once occupied by the ancient kingdom of Wuli.

They're traditionally farmers, growing groundnuts and cotton as well as other crops, but have also distinguished themselves mostly as traders and as entrepreneurs in many areas including real estate and the diamond business in Sierra Leone; also as pottery makers and as goldsmiths. They are some of the leading businessmen in The Gambia today.

They conduct trade in local markets selling a wide variety of goods. They also take their goods to other parts of the country and have established extensive commercial networks outside Gambia.

Like most ethnic groups in West Africa, the Serahule

had a caste system around which their traditional life was organised. The vestiges of this system are clearly evident in their lives even today, mostly in the rural areas where the traditional way life has not changed much since the olden days.

Polygamy is also common among the Serahule. Arranged marriages are also common. Modernisation has done little to change the social order in the traditional society of the Serahule; a phenomenon that has also been observed in other traditional societies in The Gambia and elsewhere across the continent because of the resilient nature of African cultures. Traditional societies are the most conservative. Many of them are resistant to change even today.

The Serahule are just one example. And in spite of their minority status in The Gambia, they stand out for several reasons. According to an article, "The Serahule," in a Gambian newspaper, the *Daily Observer*:

"The founders of the ancient Empire of Ghana were the Serahule.

At its height in the early eleventh century the Kingdom of Ghana was mainly populated by the Serahule.

Serahuli society was also stratified into the nobles known as the Nore, the artisan class comprising the Jaare or praise singers, the Tagge or smiths, and the Garauke or leather workers.

At the bottom of the social ladder were the slave class known as the Komme and also consisting of domestic and commercial slaves.

As middlemen in the trans-Saharan trade, as we shall see, the Serahule grew wealthy and became great traders.

With the conquest of Ghana in the eleventh century by the Almoravids, the trans-Saharan trade got disrupted and the trade routes shifted from Serahule territory. The Almoravid conquest of Ghana and the resultant loss of fortune by the Serahule contributed in their dispersal into other parts of West Africa.

Although they were not permanent residents for the most part, the Serahule were found scattered in many Gambian districts with their largest concentration in the Upper River Division of The Gambia.

The Serahule had long been associated with the Mandinka as long distance traders from Senegal and Upper Niger regions. Coming from the Senegal valley to The Gambia, they would hire land from the Mandinka chiefs and grow groundnuts for a few years, just long enough to be able to buy the goods they wanted from the European traders before returning home.

Of course the Serahule were predominantly traders, but they also engaged in farming. They grew groundnuts and cotton and their women folk are noted for manufacturing decorated clay pots.

By the middle of the nineteenth century, the Serahule, mobile and without local ties, proved themselves useful to the local Gambian kings as mercenaries and were paid out of the profits from the raids which they undertook. In Numi, for example, Demba Sonko, King of Niumi, during the 1850s, hired a band of 700 Serahule to maintain order within the kingdom and exact custom duties from its rebellious eastern districts.

Despite being a minority ethnic group in The Gambia, however, the Serahule are today among the leading entrepreneurs of the country and have contributed immensely in its economic activities through their skills as renowned traders." – (Dawda Fall, "The Serahule," in the *Daily Observer*, Banjul, The Gambia, 19 February 2008).

The entrepreneurship of the Serahule is also clearly evident in their traditional society in which roles are clearly defined in a stratified or hierarchical way.

They have blacksmiths, leather workers, carpenters, and so on, each occupying a special place in the traditional society. As in most traditional societies in West Africa, the

Serahule also have praise singers known as *jaroo* in their language.

But in spite of their reputation as traders, their society has relied mostly on farmers to sustain it.

Customs and traditions play a central role in their lives. Most of them are Muslim but they also practise traditional beliefs. One of the most important rituals is circumcision, a practice demanded by both Islam and the traditional society.

One of the main reasons Islam was able to spread among the Serahule and other indigenous groups was its conformity with a number of traditional practices such as circumcision and polygamy.

Gender roles are another feature of Serahule traditional society. Men usually work on the farms while women take care of the children and the household.

Serahule women are also known for dyeing cloth. In fact, dark blue indigo is identified with the Serahule. They consider it to be an integral part of their identity as a people. It's also identified with their traditional society.

The rock foundation of this society is the extended family as is the case among other groups in The Gambia and elsewhere across Africa. Age seniority and gender also play a very important role in the extended family and in society as a whole.

Even when the Serahule migrate to other countries, they rely on a network of families and on the extended family to support each other. But they also face a lot of problems when they're so far away from home, as their lives in Catalonia, Spain, clearly show; documented in a work edited by Professor Russell King, director of the Sussex Centre for Migration Research at the University of Sussex, *The Mediterranean Passage: Migration and New Cultural Encounters in Southern Europe*:

"In the Gambia, the whole ethnic representation – dominantly Mandinka, followed by Fula, Wollof, Jola,

Serahule and Serer – has been reproduced by their geographical concentration in Catalonia.

Curiously, for both the Gambia and Morocco, the two groups which are generally considered to be the most traditional by the rest of the sending country's society – the Serahule in the Gambia and the Rifians in Morocco – are also the most numerous amongst Gambian and Moroccan migrants in Catalonia.

Both groups are characterised by higher fertility rates, a higher index of polygamous marriage and a stronger adherence to the Muslim religion compared to the norm for migrants from their respective countries.

Another form of social organisation which I observed was the reproduction of family structures, evident in all three national communities studied (the third one being Filipino).

In the Gambia the family unit expresses the microcosm of hierarchical social organisation on the criteria of age and gender.

The Serahule extended family offers a whole network of economic relations between families which are very influential in creating the support base for any migratory project.

However, once in Catalonia, this traditional family structure experiences a breakdown, with the loss of the elders' authority and, in particular, the dilution of power of the older women." – (Russell King, ed., *The Mediterranean Passage: Migration and New Cultural Encounters in Southern Europe*, Liverpool University Press, 2001, p. 32).

The traditional society of the Sarahule has been subjected to stress and strain because of migration.

Many men are away from home for long periods of time working as migrant workers and selling goods in different parts of West Africa. And as we have just seen, some are in Spain. Others are in different parts of Europe and elsewhere.

Those in Africa are usually gone for two to four years. But they're sometimes gone for even longer periods. In fact, the Soninke – or Serahule – have one of the highest migration rates in the entire West Africa.

Their absence from home has led to an increasing number of female-headed households in the countries where they come from, although the incidence rate varies from country to country.

And it's a disturbing phenomenon whose negative impact is only neutralised by the strength of the women left behind to take care of their families as heads of households in the absence of their husbands.

So, while Western civilisation and other foreign influences have played a role in weakening traditional societies and structures across Africa, some activities by Africans themselves, even when well-intentioned, have had a negative impact on their societies although in varying degrees.

Trade has always been inextricably linked with the Serahule traditional way of life; so has migration in search of employment.

But not all tribes or ethnic groups in The Gambia and in other parts of Africa have been involved in migrant work and long-distance travel to sell their goods.

Many have done that since precolonial times. And they continue to do so, restricted only by national boundaries under the modern African state. The Serahule are some of the most prominent among them.

But the impact on the families involved can sometimes be devastating.

Serer

The Serer, also known as Serere, are the sixth-largest ethnic group in The Gambia. In neighbouring Senegal, they're the third-largest.

The most prominent Serer was Leopold Sedar Senghor, the first president of Senegal who was also a poet and philosopher. The father of the second president of Senegal, Abdou Diouf, was also a Serer; his mother, Fulani.

The Serer live mostly in the central part of Senegal. In The Gambia, most of them live in the northwestern part of the country.

Their main homeland in Senegal borders Gambia. Therefore they straddle the Gambian-Senegalese border as do other Gambian ethnic groups, all surrounded by Senegal. They're also found in Guinea-Bissau and Mauritania.

They're now mostly Muslim. But like many other African tribes, they resisted conversion to Islam for a long time. Resistance by the Serer lasted from the 1200s to the 1900s.

It was a violent conflict. It disrupted social structures and forced the Serer to flee from the conflicts with the Islamic forces who were waging *jihad* to convert them to Islam. As Professor Sheldon Gellar of Hebrew University in Jerusalem and Indiana University states in his book *Democracy in Senegal: Tocquevillian Analytics in Africa*:

"When the French began their conquest of the Senegalese interior in the mid-nineteenth century, the marabouts sided with the rulers against the French. When the monarchies collapsed after a series of crushing defeats, the marabouts picked up the pieces and established their moral and spiritual authority over the Wolof populations who converted to Islam.

Islam exercised less influence in the Serer monarchies of Sine and Saloum. Though the Serer welcomed the marabouts to their realm, they steadfastly clung to their traditional African religions.

When Ma Ba launched a jihad to establish a purer form of Islam in the areas north of the Gambia River, the Serer resisted and killed him.

Their opposition to Ma Ba and the Wolof monarchies looking to maraboutic support in their struggle with the French led the Serer to seek alliance with the French.

The influence of the precolonial rulers lasted longer in the Serer monarchies that signed treaties with the French.

At the beginning of French rule, most Serer had not been converted to Islam. However, a small number of Serer, living in communities near the Atlantic coast having long ties with European traders had converted to Christianity. Leopold Sedar Senghor, Senegal's first president, was a direct descendant of these Serer Christians." – (Sheldon Gellar, *Democracy in Senegal: Tocquevillian Analytics in Africa*, Palgrave Macmillan, 2005, p.24).

After the coming of Europeans, some Serers converted to Christianity even in the interior of Senegambia, in addition to those along the coast who had accepted the new faith much earlier.

But Christians are a small minority among the Serer in The Gambia and Senegal just like in all the other indigenous ethnic groups in the region. Many Serers still follow their traditional religious beliefs.

Their conception of God, based on their traditional beliefs and different from the Islamic faith, played a critical role in fuelling their resistance against the propagation of Islam. And they were determined to maintain their freedom and independence.

Also, inextricably linked with their religious beliefs was land. As Professor Dennis Charles Galvan, Department of Political Science and the International Studies Programme, at the University of Oregon, states in his book *The State Must Be Our Master of Fire: How Peasants Craft Culturally Sustainable Development in Senegal*:

"The Serer were...pagan and fiercely independent,

especially with regard to Islam – even though this geenralization failed to apply very well to Saluum.

The Serer were also good, indeed ideal, peasants in that their religion and culture made them especially attached to the land and especially disposed to 'husband' natural resources – even though this really only came close to being true in the Siin.

The Serer were classic egalitarian peasant traditionalists with strong circuits of reciprocity and gift exchange to even out potential imbalances in wealth – even though both centralized states were rigidly stratified in caste terms.

The rise of Islamic – primarily Mouride – peanut plantations made the Serer an even more compelling Other for the French." – (Dennis Charles Galvan, *The State Must Be Our Master of Fire: How Peasants Craft Culturally Sustainable Development in Senegal*, University of California Press, 2004, p. 43).

The Serer in The Gambia are ethnically and culturally linked to the Serer in Senegal, only separated by national boundaries drawn by the colonial rulers.

The Serer are also closely related to the Wolof and the Mandinka or Mandingo. According to a work edited by Professor Roland Oliver, *The Cambridge History of Africa, Volume 3, c. 1050 – c. 1600*:

"Even the Guelowar royal clan of the Serer states, north of the Gambia, claim descent from Malinke warriors who hailed from Kabu." – Roland Oliver, ed., *The Cambridge History of Africa, Volume 3, c. 1050 – c. 1600*, Cambridge University Press, 1977, p. 456).

Serers also have Fula ancestry with whom they have intermingled for centuries. Fulas also have Serer ancestry in varying degrees as much as they do other ancestries including Serahule, Wolof, Mandingo and others; a strong testament to the intermingling that has taken place in the region of Senegambia for centuries.

The ethnic identification of the Serer – who can't be separated since they're a collective entity transcending national boundaries between Senegal and Gambia – also needs clarification. As Professor Leonardo A. Villalón, Political Science Department, University of Florida-Gainsville, who also once served as director of the Centre of African Studies at that school, states in his book *Islamic Society and State Power in Senegal: Disciples and Citizens in Fatick*:

"The label 'Serer' has long been applied to several different groups, some of which speak unrelated languages.

The 'true' Serer, who make up over 90 percent of the population identified by that name, are comprised of the speakers of Serer–Siin and the closely related Serer–Niominka, fishermen who inhabit the coastal islands north of the Gambia river and who are consequently known as *seereer-u-ndox*, or 'water Serer' in Wolof.

The most significant of the distinct small groups also called Serer are the Non, Ndut, and Safene (sic) peoples who inhabit a series of villages around the region of Thies. Because their numbers are quite small, however, and given their proximity to the major urban centers, these groups seem to be especially affected by the phenomenon of Wolofization.

In a strict sense, therefore, the term Serer refers to the people who constituted the majority of the population of the traditional states of Sine and Saloum, as well as a significant minority in Baol.

Today the Serer comprise the third largest ethnic group in Senegal, and the majority of the population of Fatick." – (Leonardo A. Villalón, *Islamic Society and State Power in Senegal: Disciples and Citizens in Fatick*, Cambridge University Press, 1995, pp. 51 – 52).

And according to Professor Eric S. Charry of Wesleyan University in his book *Mande Music: Traditional and Modern Music of the Maninka and Mandinka of Western Africa*:

"The term 'Serer' encompasses several groups associated with the states of Sin and Salum, situated between the former Wolof states in the north and the Mandinka Kabu states in the south.

Although some Serer may have originated in their present region, others probably migrated from Takrur in the north beginning in the eleventh century, being pushed south by Moors, Fulbe and Jolof.

By the fourteenth century the powerful state of Sin was established, led by a line of rulers of Mandinka origin known as Gelwar.

The Salum kingdom was established in the late fifteenth or early sixteenth century by Mbegan Ndur (Ndour)." – (Eric S. Charry, *Mande Music: Traditional and Modern Music of the Maninka and Mandinka of Western Africa*, University of Chicago Press, 2000, p. 21).

And like most of their fellow countrymen, the vast majority of the Serer live in the rural areas.

They're mostly farmers, growing groundnuts and millet as well as other crops, and also own livestock, mostly cows. But they're also known to be very good fishermen.

Like the other groups in Senegambia, the Serer traversed vast expanses of territory during precolonial times and saw the entire region as their home, as their history of migration in the area clearly shows.

They have a long history in the region of Senegambia and have intermingled with other groups for centuries, intermarrying and exchanging cultural knowledge, and even customs and traditions. Yet they have, at the same time, retained their own identity as an ethnic group.

And in spite of their minority status in The Gambia, they stand out as an ethnic group in a number of ways. According to a Gambian newspaper, *Today*:

"The Serer are one of the smallest ethnic groups in The Gambia, but are the third-largest in neighbouring Senegal with an estimated population of just over a million.

Traditionally, they are fishermen and boat makers, but have also been proved to be great intellectuals although not so famed in The Gambia as in Senegal which has seen its first two presidents come from this tribe – the late Leopold Sedar Senghor and Abdou Diouf.

Senghore was a poet, an author and a great pan-African revered by his peers around the world.

Although staunch animist, Serers have embraced Christianity and Islam with the majority being Christians. Cardinal Theodore Adrien Sarr, a Senegalese with a family in The Gambia is also a Serer of whom both countries are proud of. Bishop Solomon Tilewa Johnson – the first Gambian to hold the post of Bishop of The Gambia is also a Serer. He is one of the most respected bishops in the Anglican diocese.

The Serer are also believed to be the original first migrants in The Gambia along with the Jola.

Today in The Gambia, they live in great numbers in the former states of Sine, Saloum, Jokadu, Barra and Niumi. They are also found in large numbers in the areas of the former kingdoms of Baol, Kayor and Jolof.

The Serer are divided into sub-groups and can have different dialects of the Serer language which may be difficult for another Serer to understand, though all dialects have the same roots.

The Origin and Founding of Serer States

The most popular belief is that the Serer migrated from Kaabu in the upper Casamance about four hundred years ago. This migration was believed to have been caused by civil war after the death of one of their kings.

War broke out between the dead king's brother and his son Boure. They both wanted to take over the throne. Boure was defeated and left the state with his supporters.

They moved northwards, passing through Foni, then across the River Gambia to Baddibu and eventually founded their first settlement, Mbissel near Juwaala (Joal) in the area that later made up the state of Sine.

Some oral historians believe that they migrated after they were defeated by Almoravid allies who were fighting for Islam, as the Serer did not want to do away with their animist beliefs. They took a stand against the great Almoravid army, were defeated, and that led to their migration to what later became to be known as Sine.

It is also believed that the Serer emerged before the Wolofs. Historians say that they were ruling Jolof before the Jaw, Ngom, Mengue and Njie dynasties.

The most notorious of the rulers generally referred to as Mansa Jolofing was a Serer well known for his dark art during the reign of Mansa Sundiata Keita of Mali. When Sundiata Keita sent his men to go to Jolof to buy horses with a caravan loaded with gold, the Mansa Jolofing ransacked the caravan, took all the gold as well as the horses.

Having found out what happened, Sundiata Keita sent his cousin and general Mansa Tiramanghan Trawally - [future conqueror of Kaabu] to Jolof to assassinate the Serer king.

Another tradition claims that the Serer settlements were later ruled by Mandinka Nyanchos who migrated from Kaaabu.

During the Serer migration, they met small groups of Mandinka whom they either incorporated into their society or defeated in battle.

The Serer decided to settle in forest areas because the environment proved favorable to their culture. The first settlements were ruled by chiefs who had the local name 'Laman.' Consequently, many Serer settled in the Wolof and northern Gambian states.

One group of migrant Mandinka intermingled with the Serer and eventually controlled them, but assimilated Serer culture and language. These Mandinka rulers came to be known as Gelowar (Gelwar) in the states of Sine and Saloum. They were Nyanchos (a branch of Kaabu ruling class). The first Gelowar ruler in Sine was known as Mansa Wali Jon with his capital at Jakhao (Diakhao).

The system of inheritance was matrilineal, as was the case in Kaabu. Thus, when Mansa Wali died, he was succeeded by his sister's son. This royal lineage was established in Sine by the end of the 14th century.

Saloum, the other Serer state, was ruled by a grand nephew of Mansa Wali Jon. He was called Mbegan Ndure. However, his position of kingship was gained through conquest rather than by inheritance. He waged a successful war against the marabouts who were at the time in control of Saloum during the latter part of the 14th century. He built a new capital called Kahone (Kawoon). The Gelowar kings ruled Sine and Saloum well into the 19th century when they were conquered by the French.

In their earlier stages, both the Sine and Saloum were vassal states of the king of Jolof, by either voluntary association or conquest. However, it was considered to be voluntary because Mansa Wali proposed the acceptance of Jolof authority. By the mid-16th century, both Sine and Saloum and other vassal states had gained their independence, especially when Kayor rebelled against Jolof political domination.

Sine and Saloum later extended their boundaries to a great extent, encompassing the states of Baol, Kayor, and Niumi which paid tribute to them. Marriage alliances were formed with kings, princes and princesses of neighbouring states.

One such alliance was the marriage between the ruler

of Kayor, Birayma Faatim-Penda, and a Gelowar woman from the state of Saloum called Kodou Joof. This marriage enabled their son to have claims to both the thrones of Kayor and Saloum through the female line. Like the Wolof states, the Serer states were almost always engaged in disputed successions, as there were many claimants to the throne.

Sine and Saloum

Sine and Saloum were separate states in west-central Senegal that were populated mainly by Serer who had migrated there between the 10th and 13th centuries. They lived in autonomous groups governed by individual chiefs and under the nominal sovereignty of the Jolof Empire.

In the 1300s, Nyancho ranchers from Kaabu settled in Sine and established a state system ruled by the descendants of a female migrant Koulaar Omeo. The Gelowar dynasty traced its descent through its matrilineal line as did the Kaabu population.

Saloum was founded by the 11th King of Sine, Mbegan Ndure who reigned from 1494 – 1514.

Its individual chiefdoms unified under the aristocracy of the Gelowar dynasty. Saloum expanded in the 1500s and gradually annexed the Mandinka Gambian kingdoms from Niumi to Niani on the north bank of the Gambian river extending as far eastward as Kaur.

The capital of Sine was Jakhao 15 kilometres northeast of Fatick-Senegal while the capital of Saloum was Kahone, 5 kilometres east of Kaolack. Both states were active in the Atlantic-oriented trade of the precolonial centuries, dealing primarily with the French merchants in bees wax, cow hide, salt and slaves. Today, the regions are prime groundnut producing areas. The Gelowar dynasty of both kingdoms lasted till the French colonialists took over the area in the late 1800s.

Lifestyle and Culture

The Serer had a 'Bur,' the highest office in the land, and was in control of state affairs and 'controlling' the forces of nature. When he became quite elderly, he was ritually killed as their belief was that he was no longer able to ensure the fertility of female members of the tribe or of livestock.

Serers are known for their love for pounded coos (chere) which is their favorite dish.

Although they are known for their expertise in farming and fishing, they are also known to be great wrestlers. They have been known to dominate the wrestling arena in the Senegambia region since its emergence.

Their traditional attire is called 'serr.' It is often woven by Serer men, and it is sometimes believed to protect those who wear it from harm. It is also believed to bring the wearer good luck.

In their festive occasions and even when an elderly person dies, they beat the 'gamba' (a big calabash with a small hollow-out). They are not known to have any masquerades though. Serer women are also known to like the idea of tattooing their chins and/or gums.

Common Serer surnames are Sarr, Joof, Faye, Ndure, Senghore and Ngum. The origin of the surname Njie [the last dynasty in Jolof] although usually associated with the Wolof tribe, is in fact Serer.

Even with their religious beliefs, most Serer are known to adhere greatly to their culture and tradition, which at times may be against the practices of their (Islamic or Christian) religion." – (Edward E. Carayol, "The Serer," in *Today*, Kanifing, The Gambia, 5 November 2009).

Another profile of the Serer in a different Gambian newspaper provided basically the same perspective but with additional details here and there; for example, the fact that as an ethnic entity, the Serer are a product of more than one race. According to the *Daily Observer*:

"Though we have described Sine and Saloum as part of the Wollof Empire at its height, the leading people of these states were the Serer.

These people also have traditions of migration into the Senegambia area, and are also believed to be the product of racial fusion between non-Negro immigrant groups and indigenous Negroes. Their customs and language bear considerable similarity to those of the Wollof.

They appear to have settled originally to the north of the Senegal but under pressure from more powerful peoples, they moved into Futa Toro and became subjects of the Tukulor.

Other invaders including Wollof, forced the Serer to migrate south westwards until they finally established themselves in small states in the Sine-Saloum area probably in the twelfth century.

The Serer states of Sine and Saloum came under Wollof domination but remained Serer in character. Both Tukulor and Mandinka invaders finally won control of Sine and Saloum and a series of smaller states along The Gambia including Niani and Wuli. The Mandinka migrants took over much of the Serer culture including their language.

They took the Wollof *bur* in preference to *mad* which was the Serer title of king.

The Serer had roughly parallel social structure as the Wollof, marked by the existence of distinct status grouping of nobles, free peasants and slave warriors, as well as castes of artisans.

The Serer can be divided into five major status groups and 'a number of sub-groupings.'

First, there was the nobility who, as in the case of the Wollof, consisted of holders of royal power and their relatives.

Second, there were the 'Tyeddo,' the warriors who largely made up the entourage of the *bur* and their major chiefs.

In the third and largest status group were the 'Jambur,' the commoners or free peasants. They participated in the political system, and their consent was necessary for its operation. A number of major chiefs were chosen from their ranks.

Fourth, came a series of castes of which the most important was the griot. Caste status were inherited and attached to an economic activity.

Griots were well-rewarded for their work and often became rather wealthy. However, the most rigid of marital taboos was against marriage with griots. They could not be buried in soil, and their corpses were generally placed in the arms of giant baobab trees.

Fifth and last on the social ladder were the slaves. Here again there were the trade slaves and domestic slaves.

The Serer did not develop any complex political institutions until they came into contact with the Guelewarr. The *bur* of both Sine and Saloum were chosen from among the Guelewarr.

In both Sine and Saloum, the *bu*r was the highest political and religious personality. He was charged with operating the state and with taming those forces beyond the control of man.

The most important factor dividing the peoples of the Senegambia was the differential impact of Islam.

In this the Serer stood out as one of the groups that had undergone no conversion.

A *bur*, who reached old age, was subject to ritual murder because it was believed he could no longer guarantee that cattle and women would remain fertile.

In theory, the oldest male Guelewarr became *bur*. In practice, the Guelewarr who could amass the most power ascended the throne. Constitutional processes merely confirmed and gave legitimacy to the most power

Guelewarr." – ("The Serer," in the *Daily Observer*, Banjul, Gambia, 25 February 2008).

    The Serer society was highly centralised, based on a caste system like most traditional societies in West Africa. The structures of this hierarchy lasted for a long time even after they were conquered by their invaders.
    The Serer society had another distinctive feature. Women who were members of the ruling families wielded political power and influence. They also exercised judicial functions unheard of in many other traditional societies which were exclusively male-dominated.
    Their stratified society was divided into seven classes. At the top was the royal class, followed – in descending order – by the nobility, warriors, servants for royal clans, artisans, and slaves.
    There were three kinds of slaves. There were those who were used to pay debts – given away as commodities or goods of exchange. There were those who worked as domestic servants and stayed with the families for whom they worked for the rest of their lives; it was a hereditary role and their children, and grandchildren, continued to work as slaves for the same families. Then there were slaves who were bought or captured in war.
    Even today, the people know which class or caste they are descended from. But the stratification is not as rigid as it was in the past, although the people are expected to know where they belong. The people in the rural areas are more likely to pay attention to that than their brethren in urban centres because of the conservative nature of the traditional society. The people in the villages are the last to change.
    Today, the Serer retain much of their old culture, customs and traditions. In fact, it's not uncommon to hear how Serer culture has survived through the centuries in spite of all the forces which tried to destroy it. According to a work edited by Professor Griselda Pollock of the

University of Leeds and Victoria Turvey-Sauron also of the same school, *The Sacred and the Feminine: Imagination and Sexual Difference (New Encounters: Arts, Cultures, Concepts*:

"It is explained and known by emic members of Senegalese society that the Serer culture is one of the cultural universes that have survived in its integrity in Senegal (and Gambia), despite all the waves of other cultures.

It is, therefore, viewed as still very strong and powerful in modern times, seen as having no tension in contemporary Senegalese society.

Women are also very powerful in Serer culture and religion both of which they totally control as women and priestesses. They are the healers, as Clement correctly tells us, and they use various ritual procedures, but what they spit over the possessed woman is not saliva as Clement reports. It is water projected from the mouth in a process the Wolof call *boussou* (the verb to spread, meaning 'that which is spread'), water that the woman healer absorbs and keeps in her mouth.

She now ritually 'spreads' the water over the possessed woman to purify her spiritual body as a patient. Since the water has come through the mouth of the initiated healer/priestess, whose mouth is now sacred, the water also is considered to have become sacred from having gained power and force through the healer...." – (Griselda Pollock and Victoria Turvey-Sauron, eds., *The Sacred and the Feminine: Imagination and Sexual Difference (New Encounters: Arts, Cultures, Concepts*, I. B. Tauris, 2008, p. 92).

There are other aspects of Serer culture, and its resilience through the centuries, elaborated here:

"The Serer are a mtarilineal people, like the Wolof and

other peoples in the Mandingo zone of the West African Sahel, who now have to process the overlays of androcentric and patriarchal religions in their world, namely the Abrahamic religions, one of which is Christianity that Kristeva describes as 'a paternal cult' and a 'cult of the father and son.'

Very perceptively she disquisitions at length on Mariology, the cult of the Virgin Mary, and shows that the Virgin Mary is constructed in such a way by the Church that she is finally not a woman at all, despite her motherhood, and not a human either, due to her ascension in Catholic doctrine. As she does not experience sex or death, Mary is beyond being human.

Due to the vital survival of Serer religious culture where women are actual, human women, however, the women at a Roman Catholic mass still try to worship their Supreme deity, *Rokh*, as they express their humanity in incantations, screaming and possession, if that state of consciousness is attained.

What transpires, therefore, is that the Serer women superimpose their *Rokh* consciousness over the Catholic liturgy; in a manner similar to the process that can be observed in voodoo – the African Diaspora indigenous religion of Haiti in which the African deities are superimposed on Christian saints as was also done in Brazil. The superimposition in Senegal is done in a way that raises the women to the level of possession. For instance, the Lord's Prayer in the Christian service may be chanted in the tones present and used only in the liturgy for Rokh worship and then raised to decibels where possession takes place.

It is subtle as this – expressing a Serer religious consciousness over Catholic substance...through the adaptation of the intonation of a Serer liturgy to a foreign one in a manner that may appear as screaming to an outsider, which the French Senegalese official himself might well be. That is, he may not himself be a Serer." –

(Ibid., pp. 92 – 93).

Then there is the question of ethnicity, and ethnic identity, which is critical to any study and understanding of African societies and cultures which are built or organised on the basis of common identity shared by a particular group of people known as tribes or ethnic groups:

"This brings us to the question of ethnicity that Clement herself proceeds to raise in relation to class.
She says the women were villagers and servants after which she makes one of her usual blanket statements about 'Africa': that 'in Africa what is so easily called 'ethnic group' also depends on the caste system – very concealed but still extremely present – as well as social roles.'
To say that what are so easily called ethnic groups in Africa depend on caste systems is a mystifying sociological statement. There may be caste systems in Senegal (and Gambia) but they do not define ethnic groups because different castes are found in the same ethnic group." – (Ibid., p. 93).

Caste is not synonymous with tribe or ethnic group. Otherwise the entire Serer, Wolof, Mandinka, Fulani ethnic groups – each one of them is a single caste or class. It's a gross misconception of African societies to equate castes with tribes or ethnic groups.
Ethnic groups or tribes do exist. They constitute traditional societies. And they in turn constitute the building blocks of the larger societies we call nations.
Traditional cultures also still exist. But they're not as dynamic, and not as influential, as they were in precolonial times.
Modersination has played a major role in undermining the social structures of traditional societies, for example, chiefdoms which were abolished in some African

countries after the countries won independence; and where they still exist, their role is very limited. In many cases, the role of chiefs today is ceremonial rather than functional.

In the context of Gambia, Serer culture, which is the focus here, still exists and has proved to be one of the most resilient through the centuries. Even those who have been linguistically Wolofised, as has happened in neighbouring Senegal, don't see that they have in any way lost their cultural identity as Serers. As David Crystal states in his book *Language Death*:

"Not all cultures...seem to have to have the same regard for language as a potent symbol of ethnic identity. Matthias Brezinger and his colleagues have reported some instances from Africa. In one paper, they describe the behaviour of several Serer men from Senegal who had replaced their language with Wolof:

> Nevertheless, they turned out to be ardent adherents of Serer culture and ethnic identity, who described Wolof culture as being 'inferior' to their own in almost all respects, insisting that they would do everything possible in order to defend Serer culture against Wolof domination.
> The fact that none of them was able to speak the Serer language was for them quite irrelevant.

Anecdotes like this underline the point that culture is multi-faceted, containing thousands of elements, many of which have nothing directly to do with language, belonging to such domains as clothing, hairstyle, food, dance, crafts, and the visual arts. It is perfectly normal for people to use these as 'badges of ethnicity,' whether or not they control the associated language. They see language as just one of the badges available to them.

Because of its complexity and pervasiveness in society, of course, language is widely acknowledged as the behaviour with the greatest potential to act as a badge; but it is not the only way that culture can be transmitted.

Culture does not come to a complete stop, when any one of its elements changes or ceases to exist, even when that is language." – (David Crystal, *Language Death*, Cambridge University Press, 2002, p. 121).

What has been observed among the Serer as cited above – and among other groups in Senegal and Gambia who have been Wolofised and Mandinkanised linguistically and even culturally in some cases – is analogous to what has taken place in Tanzania.

Many people in Tanzania, especially of the younger generation and those who have been brought up in towns and cities where communities have been linguistically detribalised, speak only Kiswahili or Swahili. It's the primary language for most Tanzanians.

And quite often, it's the only language for many of them. They don't speak any other language. They don't speak their tribal languages. Many of them don't even know their tribal languages.

They don't even know their tribal cultures, customs and traditions, let alone their tribal languages, because they're urbanised. They were born and brought up in the towns and cities where they have intermingled with members of other tribes and have become detribalised.

Yet they know what tribes or ethnic groups they belong to, and acknowledge their ethnic identities, even though it's not their primary identity in a country like Tanzania where there has been a heavy emphasis on the promotion of national identity at the expense of tribal identities, with Kiswahili or Swahili being one of the tools used to achieve this goal.

I am a typical example of that myself. I have not spoken my tribal language, Kinyakyusa, also known as Nyakyusa, in almost 40 years now and am no longer fluent in it as I am in Kiswahili. Yet, I have not lost my ethnic identity as a Nyakyusa simply because the only African language I speak is Kiswahili and I can no longer speak my tribal language fluently.

Nyakyusa is not even my primary identity. I am a Tanzanian first, then Nyakyusa next. But I have not lost my ethnic identity as a Nyakyusa. The fact that I speak only Kiswahili does not mean I'm no longer a Nyakyusa.

Had I lived in Tanzania all those years; and had I been around other Nyakyusas or had been able to spend sometime in our tribal homeland in the Great Rift Valley in the Southern Highlands in southwestern Tanzania, I still would be able to speak Kinyakyusa or Nyakyusa today.

But even then, I still would not have considered myself to be a Nyakyusa first and a Tanzanian next. I still would have considered myself to be a Tanzanian first and a Nyakyusa next as is the case with most Tanzanians who consider themselves to be Tanzanians first and Pares, Safwas, Nyikas, Zaramos, Nyakyusas, Ziguas, Fipas – whatever they're ethnically – next.

I have been Swahilised linguistically just as most Tanzanians have been.

Also, many educated Tanzanians – and Kenyans – speak Kiswanglish, a mixture of Kiswahili and English, incorporating English words and phrases into Kiswahili. There is even some speculation that Kiswanglish could become a lingua franca in Tanzania and Kenya especially as more and more people learn English, enabling them to use English words and phrases, freely, together with Kiswahili.

Kiswanglish is therefore also playing an important role in detribalising many people in Tanzania, although not as much as Kiswahili does since not all Tanzanians know English as much as they do Kiswahili.

That is not the case in Kenya. Kiswahili and Kiswanglish don't play the same role in Kenya as they do in Tanzania, detribalisng people, because tribalism is so deeply entrenched in Kenya, and is so rampant, that it has become a national institution and a "virtue" to be cherished.

That is in sharp contrast with Tanzania where Swahili, or Kiswahili, has played a critical role as a force of integration, helping to create a cohesive national entity – out of 130 different tribes – unparalleled on the African continent.

In fact, speaking one's tribal language in front of other people who don't know the language or who are not members of one's tribe and identifying oneself on the basis of one's tribal identity – saying I am a Nyakyusa, I am a Ngoni, I am a Nyamwezi, I am a Hehe, I am a Nyaturu and so on – is frowned upon in Tanzania. It's also considered to be rude and tribalistic.

Yet, tribal or ethnic identities and cultures still exist in Tanzania. And they're still strong. They're also preserved and promoted in their own contexts but not at the expense of national unity which transcends tribal identity.

In the case of The Gambia, ethnic cultures have also been subordinated to a higher culture. They do exist as Serer, Mandinka, Fula, Wolof, Serahule, Jola, Manjago, and so on. And they're still strong. But Islam has prevailed as the main culture in the country as a whole. It's analogous to the dominance of the Swahili language in Tanzania as a unifying factor.

Islam is, for all practical purposes, the national culture, hence a way of life for most Gambians in the urban and in the rural areas.

Also, many tribal laws which in traditional societies fostered and perpetuated inequalities and even held some people in bondage have been abolished in this era of modernisation. Everybody now is under the same law.

Some people may bemoan all this, but there are many who celebrate the virtues of modernisation without necessarily condemning the past in its entirety.

Aku

The Aku constitute one of the smallest ethnic groups in

The Gambia together with the Manjago, the Bambara and a few others. They're also unique in the country.

Among all the groups in The Gambia, the Aku stand out in one fundamental respect. They are of black African origin. Yet they don't belong to any particular tribe.

Some of them are descended from Africans – such as the Yoruba, the Igbo, the Fanti, the Ewe and others – who were rescued from slave ships after the slave trade was abolished. But they lost their tribal identities through intermarriage which has taken place through the years since the 1800s.

Also known as Krio or Creole, the Aku are detribalised Africans who are a product of many African tribes or ethnic groups and now have their own identity as an ethnic group.

They even have their own language based primarily on English Creole which has incorporated words from some African languages such as Yoruba. It has even borrowed a few words from French and Portuguese.

The language of the Aku, which is also known as Aku, is similar to Krio – or Creole – spoken in Sierra Leone, especially in Freetown.

The Aku have an interesting history just like the rest of their fellow countrymen But it did not start in The Gambia. As a group, there were no Aku in The Gambia before the Krio migrated there in the 1800s.

The "roots" of the Aku can be traced to Sierra Leone where descendants of African slaves found a home after their harrowing experience working as beasts of burden in Britain. A few came from other parts including Canada and the British West Indies.

Those who came from the United States included soldiers who supported the British against the Americans who were fighting for independence. The British promised them freedom if they helped them fight against the American revolutionaries.

Among those who settled in Sierra Leone were

Africans who were freed from slave ships bound for America after the slave trade was abolished. Together with the freed slaves, they formed a community in Sierra Leone which came to be known as Krio or Creole.

The British started moving some of them from Sierra Leone to The Gambia in the 1830s to find more settlement areas for them. The first arrivals settled in Bathurst near the coast, and Georgetown now known as Janjanbureh, farther inland in what is now the Central Division.

The new settlers had skills the indigenous people did not have, giving them an advantage they exploited skillfully to stay ahead of the natives. I use the word "natives" in the context of its original meaning, not as a derogatory term; its derogatory connotations being a product of racism and imperial arrogance.

The Aku themselves had already acquired some of these traits from the Europeans and felt they were better than the natives whom they considered to be backward, ignorant and primitive, even incapable of performing some of the most rudimentary tasks. They were, in many respects, whites with a black skin.

But the situation was not comparable to that of Liberia where free slaves from the United States who came to be known as Americo-Liberians dominated the country and even engaged in virtual slavery.

In the 1930s, the Americo-Liberian government sent native Liberians to work in Spanish Equatorial Guinea in West Africa, and in Panama as well as other parts of Latin America on contracts which amounted to selling them into slavery.

And within Liberian itself, Americo-Liberians mistreated and exploited the indigenous people and used them as virtual slaves; an injustice which continued until 1980 when soldiers who were members of the native tribes overthrew the government, ending 150 years of Americo-Liberian domination of the country.

A lot has been written about this contract labour

scandal. The domination and exploitation of the indigenous people by the Americo-Liberians is also well-documented.

I have also written about it in some of my books including *Military Coups in West Africa Since The Sixties*:

"The contract labor scandal involved the conscription of members of the indigenous tribes to work as laborers under conditions which amounted to slavery on the island of Fernando Po (now Bioko) in the Spanish African colony of Equatorial Guinea, in Panama and other Latin American countries.

The contract was between the Americo-Liberian dominated government and the Spanish authorities. They paid the Liberian government for the labor, while the 'native' laborers got virtually nothing. Many of them died as virtual slaves, especially in Panama and on the island of Fernando Po.

The contract labor scandal also involved forced labor extracted from the 'natives' who were forced to work, without pay, on public works and other government projects – and even for Americo-Liberian families – within Liberia itself.

Tubman's regime, like those of his predecessors, owed much of their prosperity – and that of the Americo-Liberian community – to this enslavement of their fellow countrymen who were mistreated for no other reason than that they were considered to be inferior to the 'civilized' descendants of the freed American slaves who settled in Liberia.

And like his predecessors, Tubman continued to perpetuate this myth of Americo-Liberian superiority, despite his vaunted policy of 'unification' of the settler (Americo-Liberian) and indigenous communities.

In fact, it was Tubman himself who, during the 1950s and 1960s, made trips to the Caribbean to encourage Jamaicans and other islanders – and appealed to black

Americans as well – to migrate to Liberia in order to enlarge the settler community, consolidate its power, and spread 'civilizing' influence among the 'primitive natives' who were considered by many, if not by the majority, of the Americo-Liberians to be a despicable lot." – (Godfrey Mwakikagile, *Military Coups in West Africa Since The Sixties*, Huntington, New York: Nova Science Publishers, Inc., 2001, p. 91.

See also Godfrey Mwakikagile, *The Modern African State: Quest for Transformation*, Huntington, N.Y.: Nova Science Publishers, Inc., 2001, p. 13; G. Mwakikagile, Pretoria, South Africa, 2007; *Relations Between Africans and African Americans: Misconceptions, Myths and Realities*, New Africa Press; G. Mwakikagile, Dar es Salaam, Tanzania: *Africans and African Americans: Complex Relations, Prospects and Challenges*, 2009).

And as Dr. Amos Sawyer, an Americo-Liberian, who once served as dean of the school of social sciences at the University of Liberia and later as president of the interim government of national unity in Liberia from 1990 to 1994, states in his book *The Emergency of Autocracy in Liberia: Tragedy and Challenge*:

"Opposition (to Americo-Liberian rule) in the indigenous community was essentially a struggle for inclusion.

Having suffered several military setbacks (at the hands of Americo-Liberians), minimal participation in decision-making structures, an unanswered appeal to the international community, by the 1940s, the indigenous intelligentsia was resorting to efforts to organize a political party.

Failing to gain legal registration of the United People's Party (UPP), the indigenous intelligentsia then coopted a dormant but registered party known as the Reformation Party and posed the first open challenge to Tubman....

Tubman was bent on perpetuating himself in office. He did not allow the party's candidates to be listed on the ballot, charged its leaders with sedition, and disbanded it.

Sought by security forces, Didwho Twe, the party's presidential candidate, fled to neighboring Sierra Leone....

Twe had previously fled the country when, in the early 1930s, he was pursued by President (Edwin) Barclay for his opposition to the pacification campaign that followed the contract labor scandal." – (Amos Sawyer, *The Emergency of Autocracy in Liberia: Tragedy and Challenge*, San Francisco, California: ICS Press, 1992, pp. 281, and 371).

Indigenous Liberians rose up against oppression but were brutally suppressed by Americo-Liberians. As I state in *Military Coups in West Africa Since The Sixties*:

"The pacification campaign was launched by the government to suppress the 'natives' in the interior because of their opposition to forced labor.

The campaign entailed military expeditions, and was prosecuted viciously, resulting in many deaths among the 'natives' at the hands of Americo-Liberian soldiers and security forces.

As a young man, Tubman himself had participated in some of those expeditions." – (Godfrey Mwakikagile, *Military Coups in West Africa Since The Sixties*, op.cit., p. 91. See also Godfrey Mwakikagile, *The Modern African State: Quest for Transformation*, p. 13).

Brutal oppression of the members of native tribes by Americo-Liberians was one of the saddest chapters in Liberia's – and Africa's – history.

Here were a people who had themselves suffered oppression because of their race and as a people of African origin. Yet they returned to Africa to do to the indigenous people exactly the same thing their white oppressors had done to them in the Americas.

Fortunately, that was not the case in The Gambia in terms of relations between the Aku and the "natives," although there were some complaints by the indigenous people now and then, here and there, through the years.

So, there have been tensions, sometimes, between the Aku community and the indigenous people in The Gambia, but mainly in the past.

The tensions could probably be best described as an uneasy relationship between the Krio settlers – later renamed Aku – and the indigenes because of culture conflict and other differences; something that happens in all societies when two groups of people who have different backgrounds end up living together.

But the Aku in The Gambia did not reach the level of dominance that Americo-Liberians did in Liberia. And relations between the two sides – between the new Krio settlers and native Gambians – never deteriorated to the level they did in Liberia.

Still, the British colonial rulers saw these detribalised, Westernised blacks as a beacon of light and hope in the "Dark Continent" where they could play a leading role spreading Christianity, European values and Western civilisation. And many of them did just that, working as teachers, preachers, and as skilled workers in different fields, teaching the indigenous people skills they did not have.

But in spite of their Western background, they did not entirely ally themselves with the colonial rulers, although many of them did since they saw themselves as harbingers of Western civilisation in Africa.

A number of Akus played a leading role in the quest for Gambia's independence. One prominent Aku, Edward Francis Small, played this role from the 1920s when he demanded self-determination for the people of The Gambia. He's widely acknowledged as one of the fathers of Gambian nationalism. Some people consider him to be the father of Gambian nationalist politics.

The Aku also played a major role on a regional scale as leading proponents of Pan-African solidarity in West Africa agitating for independence.

And the influence they exercised in The Gambia was out of proportion to their numbers in the total population. According to Professor Arnold Hughes and Professor David Perfect in their work, *Historical Dictionary of The Gambia*:

"Aku – a name initially given to Yoruba recaptives rescued by the Royal Navy from slave ships, it was subsequently extended to cover all the recaptives' Westernized descendants in the Colony area.

The great majority lived in Bathurst, while there was a smaller community in Georgetown on MacCarthy Island.

In the Gambia, the Aku in the late 19th and 20th centuries came to exercise an influence far beyond their numbers. They adopted Western modes of living, accepted Christianity, and educated their children in Sierra Leone and Britain.

The Aku became successful traders, entered the professions, and, in the period between 1945 and independence, came to dominate many important government positions in the Gambia.

Muslim members of the Aku community were known as *Aku-Marabout*, while Wolof who converted to Protestantism were known as *Aku-Wolof*.

Owing to intermarriage with surrounding peoples and a low fertility rate, the Aku population has risen slowly in recent years....Virtually all of (them) continue to live in the Greater Banjul and Brikama districts." – (Arnold Hughes and David Perfect, *Historical Dictionary of The Gambia*, The Scarecrow Press, Inc.; Fourth Edition, 2008, p. 3).

A product of Western civilisation, the Aku even today are the most highly educated group in The Gambia. And they have played a prominent role in providing high-level manpower across the spectrum since independence. Among Gambians, they were the first to receive education and attend institutions of higher learning, especially in Great Britain.

Their historical ties to Britain are clearly evident in many ways including the names they choose. Most of their names are British. Also most of them are Christian. And their language is based on English spoken in England in the 1700s.

They also still have ties to the Krio in Sierra Leone. Many Akus and Krios have familiy ties, new and old, from marriage through the years. Many Krios who migrated to Gambia where they became Akus left relatives in Sierra Leone.

But many people even in The Gambia don't know much about the history of the Aku. Even some educated Gambians don't know much about the Aku. According to an article, "The Aku," in a Gambian newspaper, *Today*:

"A little is known or published in The Gambia about the Aku or how they came to be. Most of their historical records are not found in most Gambian literature.

It is known however that the story of the Akus is intricately webbed into the abolition of slavery in the 19th century.

However, veteran author who specializes in the history of the peoples of the Senegambia region, Patience Godwin Sonko, and Hassoum Ceesay, historian and curator at The National Centre for Arts and Culture, are valuable in piecing together a history of the Akus.

The Aku are one of the smallest ethnic groups in The Gambia consisting of only about 1 percent of the population and are the pioneers of Western education in West Africa. They were to be later called Saros in Nigeria, Aku in The Gambia, and Creole in Sierra Leone.

According to Mr. Ceesay, the Akus or better yet Creole

can be described as an aristocracy in Bathurst and Freetown.

They are referred as such because they were the first intellectuals to acquire Western education in West Africa; products of the best educational institutions such as Fourah Bay College, Oxford and Cambridge Universities respectively.

Sir Samuel Lewis, according to Ceesay, was the first black man to be knighted.

Sir Samuel John Forster, the first Gambian lawyer, graduated from Oxford in 1893. (Other Akus include) Davidson Carroll, a lawyer, and Sir John Mahoney, the first speaker of The Gambian legislature, now National Assembly.

The first black successful merchants and educationists were also Aku. S.H.O Jones who was the first Gambian Director of Medical Services was also an Aku, while the earliest African civil servants in both The Gambia and Sierra Leone were also Aku.

They were the harbingers of nationalism in Africa: Edward Francis Small (The Gambia), Bankole Bright (Sierra Leone) and Herbert Macaulay (Nigeria).

Origin of Aku/Creole People

The Aku or Creole are freed slaves and re-captured slaves who were resettled in Freetown (Sierra Leone). They could have been descendants of Mandinkas, Fulas, Jolas, Yoruba, Asante, Ibo, Mende and or other ethnicity of Western and maybe Central Africa.

They came to be known as Aku/Creole only after they were resettled in Bathurst (now Banjul, The Gambia) and Freetown (Sierra Leone).

It could be said that the abolition of slavery gave birth to the ethnic group known in The Gambia as Aku and in Sierra Leone and other parts of Western and Central Africa as Creole (Krio).

In The Gambia, Akus are mainly descendants of Creole traders and colonial officials from Sierra Leone.

Towards the end of the 18th century, many Africans were living in London. Most of them got there through slavery in the Americas and West Indies. By this time also, a few humanitarians in England had started questioning the legitimacy of the institution and were uncertain whether it was lawful under English law. One such person was Granville Sharpe.

He was to start the first re-settling or returning black slaves to Africa.

After the American War of Independence (The American Revolutionary War) in 1775 – 1783, a large number of disbanded soldiers, slaves who had been encouraged to join the British ranks during the war, on promise of freedom, also flooded London and some went to Nova Scotia, Canada. The 'Black Poor' became as numerous as to constitute a social problem in the city.

Sharpe and his supporters managed to convince the British Government to take responsibility for these people and send them back to their original continent. They were sent to Sierra Leone where 411 of them, including their girlfriends, landed in 1787.

A piece of land was obtained from King Tom, a sub-chief of the peninsular under Naimbana, the regent of Koya, ceding this land on the coast. Sharpe called the settlement 'Province of Freedom,' but the settlers called it Granville Town, in tribute to Sharpe.

A constitution was worked out which made Granville Town independent of Britain.

As with every new settlement, problems occurred and the settlement was burned, and the British government washed its hands off it.

So Sharpe and his close associates mobilized a group of close associates and formed a company called the Sierra Leone Company. The Company was however incorporated in England, and in 1791, the old site was rebuilt and renamed Freetown.

In 1792, more settlers arrived from Nova Scotia (Canada) and in the late 1790s, the Jamaicans (Maroons) also arrived and the colony grew bigger with more hands for work and more intellectuals to direct work, as the Nova Scotians had some literates among them.

The abolition of slavery however was the turning point in the history of the Aku or Creole.

By 1807, Sharpe and his associates succeeded in persuading the British government to declare slavery illegal. This eventually led the British Government to take over the settlement.

The 1807 Act amongst other things also stated that British naval vessels should capture slave ships and their owners and crew and bring them before British courts. As it was easier to do this on the coast rather than far away Britain, taking over Sierra Leone as a British Crown Colony and establishing courts there was a prudent alternative.

The British Government therefore took over Sierra Leone in 1808. A governor was sent to rule on behalf of the King of England and Vice-Admiralty courts were established to try offenders in Freetown.

Slaves captured in this way, referred to as re-captives, were therefore set free in Freetown. Many were Yoruba from Nigeria, but there were others from other parts of West Africa such as Congo and Senegal, and even the interior of Sierra Leone.

By 1808, Freetown's population was around 2000, but by 1815 it had swelled to over 6000.

Some historians believe that the overcrowded state of Freetown led the British to encourage some to settle in their other colonies in The Gambia, Nigeria and other West African British colonies, while others believe that out of nostalgia or frustration over the limited opportunities available in their new home or the unhappy experiences of some of their lot, the Creole dispersal started in 1839 and continued up to the 20th century.

They went not only into the hinterland of Sierra Leone (Protectorate) but also to other parts of Africa (The Gambia), resulting in the serious depopulation of their villages. Krio could be found as far away as the Congo in the south, east and central Africa.

Aku Migration and Settlement in The Gambia

In The Gambia, the British failed to make James Island a colony because of French rivalry, unprofitable trade, the poor state of the island and poor climatic conditions.

The abolition of the slave trade by the British in 1807 led to the need to end the trade in The Gambia.

In 1816, Alexander Grant bought an Island (originally called Banjulo) from the King of Kombo and renamed it St Mary's Island.

Despite the fact that the island is below sea level and was often waterlogged, it was strategically located to help the British monitor the estuary of the river and see slave ships trying to enter or leave the river.

The nucleus of the settlement was called Bathurst after the secretary for the colonies, Lord Bathurst. British merchants from Britain and Senegal (Goree Island and St Louis) were encouraged by Alexander Grant and Governor Charles MacCarthy to settle in the new colony.

The British augmented the population of Bathurst by bringing in re-captives (recaptured during the journey to slavery) and freed slaves (saved and freed from slavery).

Freed slaves included pure blacks and people of mixed races who were earlier settled in Freetown. These freed slaves consisted of three groups, namely the Black Poor from Britain, Nova Scotians from Nova Scotia in Canada and Maroons from Jamaica.

There was initial mistrust between the liberated slaves and the re-captives, as the liberated slaves could not speak the local languages and dressed like the Europeans whilst the re-captives were considered uncivilized. However, their hard work, determination and successes led them (the re-captives) to be later accepted by the freed slaves.

These two groups of people sometimes became indistinguishable to many people and many among them intermarried and inter-mingled. They referred to themselves as Creole. This was true especially of wealthy liberated African and freed slaves, many of whom were staying in the capitals: Freetown and Bathurst.

Like the freed slaves who were given European names, the liberated Africans also took Christian names when they converted to Christianity.

Unlike the freed slaves who spoke broken English, the re-captive Africans could neither speak the local languages of The Gambia and Sierra Leone nor the English language.

Thus both the Creole and Aku of Freetown and Bathurst developed the Krio and Aku languages.

Although a large number of words came from the English language, there are words from other European languages, such as Portuguese and French. Languages from West African groups like Asante and Fante but especially Yoruba also formed part of the vocabulary of the Krio and Aku languages.

By 1831, a large number of liberated Africans arrived in The Gambia especially from Sierra Leone as a result of the work of the anti-slavery squadrons. Some were brought to help carry out civic works in the settlement and were returned to Freetown after the completion of their work.

Other liberated Africans were brought from Sierra Leone to help reduce the influx of liberated Africans in Freetown and its environs.

As they arrived, they settled first in Bathurst (Banjul), MacCarthy Island (Janjanbureh) or British Kombo. Many engaged in farming and other trades. Some became masons, painters, and others engaged in other businesses.

This migration to and from Sierra Leone and The Gambia of Aku or Oku marabout and Creole, explains their close affiliation.

Rise of the Aku

The Akus were not only revered intellects, but also had successes in trading and became very successful merchants. They became very rich and practically owned most of the land in Bathurst.

Some Aku and Creole merchants such as Messrs H R Carrol, Thomas Crown, William Goddard, William Forster and Charles Bocock to name a few, set up well-established retail and wholesale businesses. They imported European good and purchased groundnut, palm kernels and other African products from the Protectorate area. These were either sold to European firms or exported directly to Europe.

Yet other Creole and Aku merchants established links with West African countries and imported shea butter, gari, Atari pepper, lappa, kola nuts and other goods required by the Gambian community.

In short, they took active part in the import, export and retail trade. Aku and Creole women were mostly engaged in petty trading. As a result, legitimate trade was strengthened in the colony of Bathurst.

The first Aku town was Mocam Town (Half Die), but as the population density increased they moved to New Town, presently Banjul Central, where they had a lot of land and property.

They were also the first blacks in West Africa to receive Western education and to be part of the government and civil service. In The Gambia, the first qualified doctors, lawyers, nurses and accountants were Aku.

Among them were Mr. H.K Monday Snr, a mayor of Banjul; Mr H.K Monday Jnr, first Governor of Central

Bank and First Permanent Secretary of Finance; Mr. Valentine, the first Gambian high commissioner to London; Mr. S.H M Jones, first Gambian Director of Education; Lenrie Peters Snr, editor of *The Gambia Echo* (also renowned author) and a lot more.

Lifestyle and Traditions

Creole culture is unlike that of all other ethnic groups in Sierra Leone, and it is typical of Westernized cultures and ideals. The Creoles came to be called so in Sierra Leone and other African countries but the name Aku is only reserved for descendants of Creole people in The Gambia.

Where 99 percent of the freed slaves were Christians, some of the re-captives even though with Christian names stuck to their Muslim faith. They came to be known as the Oku (or Aku) Marabout in The Gambia.

As most of the freed slaves at one point lived in England, Nova Scotia, The West Indies and the United States of America, their eyes were already open to Western culture and civilization. So the well-to-do Akus built houses that resembled those in the Western world. They built wooden houses with stone cellars and staircases in the tradition of the places they had been to, either to live in or let to Europeans.

The re-captives some of whom were also educated and successful also followed suit.

The dress code of the Akus

Coats, hats, blouses and skirts are Western-influence, which they inculcated in their way of life. They are sometimes referred to as Black Englishmen. Even in celebrating marriage and death, western traditions are observed.

An Aku man is given the chance to court a woman, be

engaged and then get married in the same way as a Westerner. When an Aku dies (in Christianity) one is washed, clothed and laid to be viewed by family and friends, before being buried. A day charity, a seven-day or a fortieth-day charity could be held.

The Aku in The Gambia had a few masquerades of their own, the hunting devil which is originally from Sierra Leone, The Fairy (Masquerade played mostly during marriages), and another one called 'Pakin' which is from Nigeria.

The favorite dish of The Aku is 'foo-foo,' a dough-like paste made of cassava pounded into flour, and 'plasas', a spicy leafy green soup with meat and cow belly. Akus were also the first blacks to bake cakes and other pastries."
– (Edward E. Carayol, "The Aku," in *Today*, Kanifing, The Gambia, 12 November 2009).

The Aku were featured in another Gambian newspaper, providing another perspective on their history. It's essentially the same history but with additional details here and there. According to the *Daily Observer*:

"One of the results of the Trans-Atlantic Slave Trade was the emergence of a district ethnic group along the West Coast of Africa generally referred to as the Creoles, with a Krio language spoken throughout the region.

The Creole is said to derive from the Yoruba word 'akiriyo', meaning 'these who go about paying visits after a church service.' In The Gambia, the Creoles are known as the Akus.

The origin of the Akus dates back to the late eighteenth century and first half of the nineteenth when their ancestors, a number of groups of freed slaves, were landed in Sierra Leone.

The first batch of settlers to be landed were freed black slaves who had been living in England and sent to settle in Sierra Leone in 1787. The original settlement, known as the Province of Freedom, was the beginning of Freetown, the present capital of Sierra Leone.

Some of the settlers were discharged soldiers and sailors who had served with the British forces during the American War of Independence. Others were former slaves who had escaped from their American masters. Many of these people congregated in London unemployed and destitute.

It was for this reason that the British Government agreed to suggestions that they be sent to found a new home of their own in Africa, and so it was that this first batch of settlers landed in the 'Province of Freedom' in May 1787.

In 1792, new settlers were to join the settlement from Nova Scotia. These were former slaves who had fought for the British in the American War of Independence and settled in Nova Scotia by the British.

By 1800, a group of Maroons also joined the settlers from Nova Scotia. The Maroons were former slaves who had revolted against their owners in Jamaica and set up their own state. They were defeated by the British who sent them first to Nova Scotia and then to the Province of Freedom.

The number of these settlers were to be increased considerably by another group known as the 'recaptives.' These were men and women rescued from ships that were carrying them to be sold as slaves despite the formal abolition of the slave trade and slavery.

Ship loads of these recaptives were constantly landed in the area and by 1811 they outnumbered the Nova Scotian and Maroon settlers combined. These recaptives originally came from the countries throughout West Africa from The Gambia to the Congo. Few of them came from East Africa.

By the middle of the nineteenth century this mixture of settlers and recaptives had blended into a distinct cultural group. Without a common language of communication they would invent the Krio language which, based on European languages, was developed under the influence of the recaptives own various African languages including that of their neighbours, the Temne and Mende.

Cut off geographically and spiritually from their community-based ancestral religions, and unable to perform their own rites, they embraced the Christian preachers in their midst. They took new names and began to wear European-styled clothes.

Realising the practical advantages education and technical skills could offer them, they were ready to learn and see to it that their children also learned the white man's culture and civilisation. Through hard work as tailors, masons and blacksmiths, they would earn enough capital to give their children the education which would prepare them for important positions in trade and commerce.

Sir Charles MacCarthy, who was Governor in Sierra Leone from 1814 to 1824, saw the settler community in Sierra Leone as a people who could advance the prevalent European view that what Africa needed was Christianity and European civilisation.

He proposed that the Colonial Government and Christian missions should cooperate to transform them into a Christian population who would spread Christianity and European ways throughout West Africa.

As a result of missionary activities, Western education flourished in Sierra Leone. Indeed, mission schools were started since the founding of the settler colony in 1787.

By the 1840s there was a large network of primary schools, and grammar schools for boys and girls were established.

From 1876, Fourah Bay College, founded in 1827, was empowered to award degrees of the University of Durham. As a result of this investment in education, a distinguished body of Aku professional men emerged.

Among this body of distinguished professionals were

men like John Thorpe who became the first West African to qualify as a lawyer in 1850; Samuel Ajayi Crowther who became the first West African Christian Bishop in 1864, and James Africanus Beale Horton who qualified at Kings College, London, as West Africa's first medical doctor in 1859.

Meanwhile the small Sierra Leone colony offered only limited scope for this ambitious and enterprising population whilst all along the coast of Africa their skills were in demand. They found jobs as clerks and agents for European exporters or set up as exporters on their own.

As missions spread they found jobs as pastors ad teachers. Their skilled tradesmen built and repaired houses in the growing coastal towns of West Africa.

By the middle of the nineteenth century Akus were scattered in communities from The Gambia to Fernando Po, forming distinct societies widely apart from the indigenous inhabitants they preferred to Call 'natives.' Indeed, for the whole of their history the Akus had thought of British West Africa as one unit.

In the case of The Gambia, the British had, in the 1830s, sponsored a large-scale immigration of the sick recaptives and criminals not wanted in Sierra Leone society to Bathurst (Banjul) and to Janjangbure in the Central River Division.

As in Sierra Leone, some outstanding Akus emerged in The Gambia. One such leading Gambian Aku was Thomas Joiner.

Joiner was a Mandinka griot born about 1788 who was captured and sold into slavery in the Americas. He was to work hard and bough his freedom. He worked as a steward on a boat sailing to West Africa. On reaching The Gambia, he left the boat and started a new life as a trader and soon became a prosperous merchant and ship owner.

Another prominent Aku was Thomas Rafell, an Igbo recaptive, who settled in The Gambia in the early 1820s as a discharged soldier. Having been wounded in the Anglo-

Niumi Wars he was granted a pension of four dollars a month by the British.

He also became a successful businessman. He used his wealth and influence to establish, in 1824, an Igbo Social Society which became a very active watchgod on British colonial administration in The Gambia, especially in matters affecting the welfare of the people.

Perhaps the most outstanding Gambian Aku has been Edward Francis Small who, as well shall see, was the doyen of modern Gambian politics.

Indeed the Aku community in The Gambia, as their counterparts in other West African colonies, became the first vigorous advocates of a modern nationalism whose concepts were to spread not only in West African but throughout the whole African continent.

However, with Independence and political power being assumed by the indigenous peoples of the societies in which they settled, and forming small minorities in such societies, the Akus became a submerged people." – ("History Corner – Peoples of The Gambia: The Akus," *Daily Observer*, Banjul, The Gambia, 22 January 2008).

Yet, in spite of their small size, the Aku are one of the most dynamic and most influential groups in The Gambia, a country whose foundation they helped to build as a modern African nation.

Even during colonial times, they played an important role in facilitating colonial administration when they served as clerks and as low-ranking officials subordinate to their British masters. They also helped to spread British culture and propagate Christianity.

They had the education and skills needed by the colonial administrators to help run the country and spread Western values including education in the Anglo-Saxon tradition. They also served as soldiers of the British empire. As Charles A. Coulumbe states in his book *Rum: The Epic Story of the Drink That Conquered the World*:

"The Creoles of Sierra Leone and the Aku of Gambia...built Anglican churches and schools, spoke English perfectly – as well as their own pidgin, Krio – and in all things conducted themselves as English.

They replaced the often sickened whites in the rank and file of the Royal Africa Corps, the body of troops the Crown established to defend its West African outposts." – (Charles A. Coulumbe, *Rum: The Epic Story of the Drink That Conquered the World*, Citadel, 2005, p. 133).

The role they played in those areas is inextricably linked with their history and how they came into existence as an ethnic group in both Gambia and Sierra Leone.

As in Sierra Leone, Creoles in The Gambia where they're known as Aku are the only group whose culture is mostly Western. They're also the only group with the largest number of people – in terms of percentage – who speak English, in addition to Aku.

And they're the only group with the largest number of Christians in terms of both percentage and raw numbers in a predominantly Muslim country where Islam is a *de facto* state religion.. As Dr. Omar A. Touray states in his book *The Gambia and The World: A History of The Foreign Policy of Africa's Smallest State, 1965 – 1995*:

"The constitution of The Gambia does not specify a state religion, but more than 85 per cent of Gambians are Sunni Muslims by faith.

Though Islam was introduced as early as the twelfth century, it was not until the Soninke-Marabout Wars of the mid-1850s that most of the population was converted to Islam.

Christians are estimated to constitute less than 10 per cent of the population, concentrated in the capital, with the Aku constituting the bulk of the Christian population.

It is estimated that about 1 per cent of the population

follow traditional African religion." – (Omar A. Touray, *The Gambia and The World: A History of The Foreign Policy of Africa's Smallest State, 1965 – 1995*, Hamburg, Germany: Institute of African Affairs, 2000, p. 15).

Another Gambian scholar, Professor Lamin O. Sanneh of the History Department and Divinity School at Yale University, contends that the people who constituted the core of the original Aku community were Yoruba Muslims. They were obviously surpassed by Christians through the years as the community continued to grow. As he states in his book *The Crown and the Turban: Muslims and West African Pluralism*:

"The nucleus of the Aku may have been Yoruba Muslims, but it is obvious that their number included Creole Christian converts.

I do not know of any satisfactory explanation of how in fact this Yoruba nucleus was able to preserve its language and culture on slave plantations, particularly if dispersal of slaves was a feature of plantation life.

If Aku is taken to mean Yoruba and that in turn is taken to mean Muslim, how does one designate Yoruba Christians among the Creole population?

Michael Banton hints at the difficulty in linguistic terminology when he writes: 'Perhaps 5,000 Creoles would today describe themselves as Aku though the number who can speak Yoruba is much less.' (*West African City*, London: Oxford University Press, 1957, p. 153).

In other words 'Aku' in fact comprises more than Yoruba-speaking Muslims. In the Gambia Aku is used to describe the entire Creole community, Christian and Muslim, with the latter being distinguished as Aku-Marabout." – (Lamin O. Sanneh, *The Crown And The Turban: Muslims And West African Pluralism*, Westview Press, 1996, p. 250).

There may be a plausible explanation of how the Yoruba Muslims who constituted the nucleus of the Aku community and whom Professor Sanneh talks about were able to preserve their language and culture and even their religion of Islam.

They probably did not even reach America where they would have been dispersed as slaves, making it impossible for them as a group to retain their language, culture and religion; unless they all, fortuitously, ended up on the same plantation or plantations, which is highly unlikely; or they somehow miraculously regrouped – from different plantations – on American soil before being sent back to Africa, which is also highly unlikely.

Most likely, these Yoruba Muslims were recaptives from slave ships which left Lagos, Nigeria, on their to way to America but were intercepted by the British who rescued the captured Africans – before they reached America – and returned them to the continent where they helped them to settle, first in Sierra Leone where they came to be known as Creoles or Krios, and then some of them in The Gambia where they became Akus.

The Krios who migrated from Sierra Leone to The Gambia obviously included some of these Yoruba Muslims and some Christians who together formed the first community of Akus in The Gambia. As time went on, they were joined by other settlers most of whom converted to Christianity because of British influence since The Gambia was, like Sierra Leone, under British control.

And because they were a product of cultural fusion – between British cultural elements and elements from indigenous African cultures of Yorubas and others who were rescued from slave ships as well as others who were detribalised Africans, the Aku influenced the course of Gambian history in a way other ethnic groups did not.

This influence is felt even today, especially in the capital Banjul and its surroundings where most Akus live, as clearly demonstrated by the Western way of life –

infused with cosmopolitan elements – that's prevalent in the Greater Banjul area.

In many fundamental ways, the Aku in The Gambia constitute an outpost of Western civilisation in a country dominated by indigenous cultures and by the Islamic faith which is itself a way of life integrated with African cultural elements in the lives of the vast majority of Gambians.

There are other ethnic groups in The Gambia. But they're relatively small. In fact, they're the smallest indigenous groups in the country.

They include the Manjago, the majority of whom live in Guinea-Bissau and Senegal; the Bambara who live mostly in Mali; and the Tukulor, also known as Tokolor – they're closely related to the Fula and are even considered to be Fula – who live mainly in Senegal, Mauritania, Mali and Guinea.

Each of those groups constitutes less than one per cent of Gambia's population.

And there are other groups which, together with the rest, constitute a highly diverse population in such a small country.

The Gambia is also known for harmonious relations among its different ethnic groups; a rare achievement on this turbulent continent where many countries have been wracked by civil conflicts some of which have been ignited and fuelled by ethnic and regional rivalries. As Gambian author, Abdoulaye Saine, professor of political science and comparative governments at Miami University, Oxford, Ohio, in the United States, states in his book *The Paradox of Third-Wave Democratization in Africa: The Gambia under AFPRC-APRC Rule, 1994-2008*:

"The Gambia's 1.5 million inhabitants are divided into several ethnic groups. The largest include the Mandinka (42 percent), Fula (18 percent), and Wolof (16 percent), while the Sarakule (Soninke), Serer, Jola, Manjago, Aku and other smaller groups constitute about 24 percent.

Approximately 90 percent of The Gambia's population is Muslim, while Christians and traditional worshippers constitute 9 and 1 percent, respectively.

Ethnic harmony rather than conflict has defined ethnic group relations in the post-independence era, and Islam has for the most part served as a unifying force.

Interethnic marriages have also played a key role in fostering relative ethnic harmony. This is aided by a tradition of institutionalized 'joking' relationships between groups to assuage conflict.

The Gambia is also home to a growing population of Africans from the West Africa subregion, mostly Christians from Nigeria, Liberia, and Sierra Leone. While their exact number is unknown, they are estimated to be 300,000 to 500,000 strong.

Their arrival in the 1980s, following conflicts in Liberia and Sierra Leone and military rule in Nigeria has infused the economy and culture with new financial capital and social dynamism." – (Abdoulaye Saine, *The Paradox of Third-Wave Democratization in Africa: The Gambia under AFPRC-APRC Rule, 1994-2008*, New York: Lexington Books, 2009, p. 3).

All the smaller groups mentioned here, including immigrants from other African countries who have settled in The Gambia through the decades especially since the 1980s, are just as important as the other groups I have covered in the book. But they're beyond the scope of this work.